What Christian Leaders are Within the Shadow of "I Do"

"The determination and courage it took for my dear friend Beverly to write this story of her life fills my heart with the greatest respect. Spending over four decades in an abusive marriage, helplessly hoping for answers as she cries out to God, while enduring the most unimaginable heartache and pain, and then finally escaping with just the clothes on her back. This book, *Within the Shadow of "I Do"*, is for all of those who have suffered at the hands of someone stronger, in hopes that their nightmares can be put to sleep forever. To God be the Glory!"

TJ Martini – Christian Author, Writer and Speaker

"Beverly is the most consistent person I've had the pleasure to know. Her supernatural and God-given ability to focus on and have faith in Him despite overwhelming and seemingly impossible circumstances has made her who she is today. Her book *Within the Shadow of "I Do"* is amazing and a must read for all."

Otto Kelly - Crisis Pregnancy Center - Board President

"Bev is so encouraging and authentic. She is a gifted communicator whose writing and speaking overflows with her love for Christ and Biblical wisdom.

Mechele LaBrie – Crisis Pregnancy Center, Center Director

"In the pages of this book, *Within the Shadow of "I Do"*, you will read of Beverly's years of abuse and how God brought her through to be healed. She shares this with you so that you too may find God's grace and healing."

Diane Harper – Author of Train Series, Nothing Between & Nothing More, Devotionals for Seniors.

"When you meet Beverly Chong for the first time, she is someone you will never forget. Her passion for Jesus is contagious. Her invigorating spirit will capture your heart and point you back to Jesus as the Author and Finisher of our faith. In her book, *Within the Shadow of "I Do"*, Beverly bravely shares her story and stands today as a witness for what Jesus can and will do, when you trust in Him."

Hoppy Sanchez – Calvary Chapel Reno/Sparks Ministry

"I know that this book, *Within the Shadow of "I Do"* will touch many others and be a lesson to all (especiallywomen) who have had difficult struggles and victorious outcomes through faith in Christ and in His strength which gives us perseverance to endure. It is so comforting to know that we are not alone and that there is hope... always hope. What a strong courageous woman Beverly is and how caring to share with us her amazing story.

Donna Di Cicilia – Marriage Counselor/Ministry

"Bev's personal story, *Within the Shadow of "I Do"*, tells of her love and commitment through the struggles, and her heartache and pain to reach triumph. She gives praise to God for what only He could do for her. Bev lives for the LORD and her faith radiates from her heart each day. You will hear Bev's heart as you read her story, and you will be encouraged."

Barb VanDyke - CPC Client Advocate and Counselor

Within

the Shadow of

"I Do"

Within
the Shadow of
" I Do "

Anoint me Lord, I'm breaking

Beverly Chong

First Printing November 2021

Editor: TJ Martini

Layout and Design: Gary Lebeck

Cover Design: Gary Lebeck

Published By Rivertree
Reno, Nevada

Printed in the United States of America
10 9 8 7 6 5 4 3 2 1

Library of Congress Cataloging-in-Publication Data

Names: Chong, Beverly, 1943- author.
Title: Within the shadow of "I do" : anoint me Lord, I'm breaking / Beverly
   Chong.
Description: Reno : Rivertree, 2021.
Identifiers: LCCN 2021042457 (print) | LCCN 2021042458 (ebook) | ISBN
   9781732145771 (paperback) | ISBN 9781732145771 (kindle edition)
Subjects: LCSH: Abused wives--Religious life. | Chong, Beverly, 1943- |
   Abused wives--Biography. | Marriage--Religious aspects--Christianity.
Classification: LCC BV4596.A2 C46 2021 (print) | LCC BV4596.A2 (ebook) |
   DDC 261.8/327092 [B]--dc23
LC record available at https://lccn.loc.gov/2021042457
LC ebook record available at https://lccn.loc.gov/2021042458

RIVERTREE

Dedication

I dedicate this book to Leah Joy,
for without her constant guidance and encouragement
and relentless refusal in accepting my drowning in a pit of despair,
this endeavor would not have materialized.
She is the one that counseled me in my grief,
instructed me in Scripture,
directed me to begin writing all that had taken place
within my four-decade failure of a marriage
and has been my sounding board and proofreader.
She is a no-nonsense, bottom line straight shooter,
with the compassionate heart of a Lion.
My heart is filled with love and adoration
for this gift from God... my sister.

My Prayer

My dear Father, I ask Your precious love
and anointing upon each and every person
who would hold this book in their hands
and allow the pages that unfold speak,
not just what my life has faced,
but more importantly hear, truly hear
what You have done in my life,
just like You want to do in theirs.
I give You me and I give You every heart listening,
asking Your perfect and divine Will be done.
In Jesus most precious name,
the Son of God, our Lord and Savior
Amen.

Table of Contents

"For I know the thoughts that I think toward you, says the Lord, thoughts of peace and not of evil, to give you a future and a hope. Then you will call upon Me and go and pray to Me, and I will listen to you. And you will seek Me and find Me, when you search for Me with all your heart."
Jeremiah 29:11-13

Introduction

As a writer, you wait for that perfect story to tell or hope to stumble onto something incredibly interesting, something so fascinating that you spend hours upon hours just thinking about how you are going to put it all together on paper. I have always enjoyed the gift of writing and have done so most of my life, and fiction seemed to fit my creativity like a glove. However, my serious committed writing didn't begin until 1990, and since then I have written many children's stories, because of my grandchildren, and also a few family and young adult stories.

I am sure there are many writers out there that can attest to the countless submissions they have sent out, as I can. Nothing published, of course, but that does not stop a true love for writing. Oh, and I have kept every rejection letter just as a trophy awarding my trying attempt to become "discovered," especially the ones that were encouraging or had been nibbled at!

At one time, I had thought about writing for the Lord, but nothing seemed to want to flow from my pen, even though I have experienced a lot in my faith walk. I remember having a conversation with my dad, many years ago, with him encouraging me to consider research in the direction of writing professionally. He felt my writing held such inspiration and as a gift from God, it was not to be taken lightly. As I remember, Dad said I needed to appreciate the gift of writing and use it to God's glory.

Now, we all know our parents think we excel above anyone else when it comes to our God-given talents, and I do mean God given. I believe God is the one that initiates our abilities, capabilities and talents and He is the one that orchestrates the many avenues that are presented to us throughout our lives. However, it doesn't mean we always pay attention when it is presented. But the thought of writing about something that holds a huge Christian format became a driving force in 2011, and all of a sudden, I found my pens kept running out of ink sooner than expected!

Many nights found restless sleep, because I would hear a sentence or phrase or have a nagging thought that had to be written down immediately or I would forget it. It was in those times that I truly feel the Lord speaks to me—in the middle of the night— when my mind has fallen into erase mode from the day's events, and I least expected it. I would quickly get out of bed and go hunt for paper and pen.

After a few times of scrambling in the dark and banging into some wall or shoe or piece of furniture—how did that get there? who put that there? —hunting for my writing paraphernalia that I got smart and placed a pen and tablet of paper on my nightstand. The topic of my writing, I knew all too well, but I initially felt it was strictly for my healing heart. I was at a point I needed some help fast, and this was the facet that my sister suggested… writing down feelings about everything I presently or had gone through for years. Whether it was the anger, sadness, disappointment, or questions that kept shooting answerless darts at my heart, it was for my mental and spiritual self-healing, unless God was to direct it for some other reason.

I know all writers can become extremely passionate about a topic that keeps pecking at them until they finally sit down and let the ink flow. And I believe it would be safe to say we all could write a book about the countless things we have learned and experienced throughout our own faith walk and how the results of all that experience has caused our faith to grow.

I'm sure you have had many answers to prayers that would blow the roof tops off in praise, not to mention miracles, of which only God can do and is still in the business of performing to our gasps of wonderment. I know I have. However, I never thought I would be writing on a topic that only happens to other people… not me, or so I thought!

Unfortunately, they say experience is the best teacher and like it or not—believe it or not—I feel there is a real need to talk about this and expose what is going on in too many marriages. I know there are a lot of books out there on the bookshelves that talk about marriage, but I would like to be a voice, in hopes of shedding needed light on something that is so prevalent in today's world; events I have experienced firsthand.

Sadly, the experiences within my marriage and the abuse that can find its tentacles wrapped tightly around the husband and wife have made me aware that I am not alone. And, though not alone, I continue to be amazed with the number of women I have spoken to through the years that share the same story—My story!

For I, the Lord your God, will hold your right hand,
Saying to you, 'Fear not, I will help you.'
Isaiah 41:13

Foreword

By Leah Bradley and KC

As I waited at the airport looking for my sister's face among all the people who just got off the plane, I was thinking about the call from her the night before when I heard her say, "I'm done, I have left him, can you pick me up?" She was afraid for her life, having been threatened so many times that if she ever left, he would kill her, but courage won over fear this time!

When I finally saw her walking towards me my heart hurt. The years of stress and fear showed in her face and body. All of 83 pounds, trying to navigate one carry-on bag, her purse, and a faint smile when she saw me. All I could do was pray, "Jesus help her."

It was a cold January morning and all she had was the clothes on her back, and open toed shoes! Thankful I remembered to put my fleece lined coat in the car for her to wear on the way to my home.

My sister needed a "safe haven" a place where she could find some peace, a place where she could just let the flood of emotions come to the surface that had pent up for so long. There were a lot of tears and a lot of praying, and all I could do was be there for her, love her, and let her get it all out. It seemed she thought that her life was all a pile of ashes.

But God said in Isaiah 61:3, *"He would give her beauty for ashes, the oil of joy for mourning, the garment of praise for the spirit of heaviness."*

Her Lord began to comfort her, and reassure her that He was with her, and He would lovingly carry her through all of this to victory.

After a few months of staying with us, I remember vividly the first time I heard her give a big belly laugh at something my husband said, and the next day I heard her laugh again! It had been so many years since I heard her laugh that I was sort of shocked! I just knew she was on her way to healing.

This is her story, her journey out of the ashes. It took great strength for her to write it, and a tremendous amount of courage to share it.

It's a story you will not soon forget... painful and heartbreaking, but oh how Jesus shines through her every word. I pray it will bless you.

Leah

Do you ever find yourself reminiscing your past? Remembering specific moments in life that didn't seem to have meaning at the time yet have total value now.

How about remembering that one person in your life who was always there for you no matter what. That one person, who always listened to you and comforted you even when they needed it more. The person that always helped you with anything at a drop of a dime, even when they had a mountain of things to do, or the person who cooked your favorite meal and made cookies for your friends that you were playing with just so you can make a good impression on them. The person who handmade your Prom dress so you stand out from everyone else.

Sometimes you don't realize how special and valuable that one person is until you get older. It just sneaks up into your mind at your most relaxed moment while sitting and drinking your coffee. Then it hits you, and you start thinking of all the times that one person was there for you.

As you put the puzzle pieces together, you now know, that one person is the one who needed comforting at that moment and someone to hear their voice. You then remember the pain and suffering they must have had all those years.

By now, you're overcome with a flood of emotions of pain, sadness, and frustration. You realize that person put aside their emotions and held it together in order to comfort you. Then you realize once again what strength and faith this person had. Faith, oh that incredible faith in our God to help get them through those rough times!

You start questioning yourself, how someone can be so strong and faithful through all they went through. Then you get the feeling that it can only be an angel from heaven. An angel disguised as my mother.

I've looked many times for her wings. I haven't found them yet. But I know one day I will.

KC

"In the beginning God...."
Genesis 1:1

Chapter 1

Who is Me?

I, like many others, love to read true to life stories. We all have one you know, so I thought I'd write mine as well. I know the focus can be on the "pretty people" you hear about on TV gossips and news or in magazines and books, and how they have gone through tragedies and failures only to succeed, some of the time. They are the "Somebody's" in life, who have a recognizable name.

Well, I am drawn to the "Nobody's" in life, like me, the ones who aren't known by the "Worlds" standard of importance. Their names don't mean anything to the majority of life's columns, but they are known by those who love them and have watched their lives break, fail, and get up again. They are also known by God Himself! That's who I am—only one of God's many kids and I know I'm "pretty people" in His eyes, just like so many of you.

This is my story! I grew up in Southern California and went to Western High School in Anaheim. Ours was a loving family, one that Daddy insisted we all go to church and worship God on Sundays and say grace before ever eating a morsel at mealtimes. Life was hard, budget stretched to accommodate all our needs, but filled with rules, responsibility, and lots of love—a family unit.

I am the eldest of four. My closest sister is three years younger than I, both of us born in October, and then mom waited four years—she always said it wasn't planned— before having another sister and a brother three years apart, both in March. Go figure! Not planned? Because daddy worked hard and mom was always sick, I, being the eldest, had to care for my siblings. It wasn't always fun, especially when I wasn't allowed to go anywhere, like to a friend's house, or even to the local store or movies, without taking my siblings with me. And wherever I took them, we would ride on my bike. My younger sister on the handlebars and youngest sister on the back fender. The three of us could be seen nearly every day peddling somewhere. Oh, life can be so cruel... or so I believed.

As I think back, my first personal prayer to God was when I was around 10 or 12 years old. In between running after a sibling, sitting them down to eat or putting them down for a nap, as well as doing all my chores, I would go outside and sit on the front porch of our home and cry, "God, please take me life." I would have rather been dead than to have to deal with what this life handed me!

Can you imagine feeling so unhappy that I found the need to pray such a request? And at such a young age? My goodness, I had no clue of what hardship was all about— or should I say hard work! That would be saved for adulthood. Maybe that's why God made us with the need to gradually grow in life, not just create us at a specific age or mentally wise, knowing everything there is to know!

Also, at the age of 12, of which was considered the right age to do so, I accepted Jesus as my Lord and Savior. My dad's brother, my Uncle Franklin, a missionary in India, who was on leave and came back to the States to visit, was the one who would hear my confession of faith. And although I knew that I was God's child, it took six more years before I would have another encounter with Him.

I had just graduated from high school and was hired at Disneyland in Anaheim as Peter Pan. Wow, my very first job! A major step into a real life of independence! I was so excited, and I can't tell you how much fun it was. I pressured my sister to give me my Peter Pan haircut ...with a double-edged razor blade! Boy was she nervous and complained, "I don't know how to cut hair", but I assured her she could do it! Who would have thought a few years later, she would attend Beauty College to become a hairdresser? Hmm, God's hands seem to always be choreographing life paths.

My supervisor had told me that Walt Disney himself, after seeing me one day at the park, was so pleased and that I was exactly what he had envisioned for someone to play the part!

Hearing that from Mr. Disney himself was an honor to say the least.

A lot of excitement surrounded that job, but there was a night that really shook my whole me, like never before. This particular night, after getting off work and returning to my locker, I realized someone had broken into my locker and stole my street clothes. I was completely dumbfounded and wondered why did they have to steal my clothes and what happened to theirs? Ahh, so young and naïve. To top it off, I was having the most miserable "time of the month" and was in no mood for this, especially when it was a brand-new dress that was stolen.

I walked out to the guard gate to call my dad and asked if he would please bring me something to wear home, as my $650 costume could not leave the premises and had to be returned to wardrobe. While standing in the California fog, at 9:30 at night, not being able to see my hand in front of my face and waiting for my dad to come and retrieve me, it happened.

All of a sudden, it was if that thick fog became a curtain, and somebody just pulled it open... and there standing in front of me was Jesus! I kid you not! He was as big as the whole sky, with a shimmering background behind Him. His arms were outstretched and inviting, and His eyes seemed to penetrate right through me to my very soul.

To say I was speechless is an understatement—a huge understatement! He was just there in all His glory. No words, no nothing. He just stared at me. It lasted for just a few moments, but long enough for me to just gasp a very emotional, "Oh!"

My dad showed up shortly after and handed me my clothes so I could change. Once I was in the car, I excitedly talked his head off all the way home about my encounter with Jesus. I remember sitting on the edge of the front sit facing him, no seatbelts in those days, and talking a mile a minute while I watched him silently cry. That was the first time I had ever seen my dad cry.

Something so amazing as this was, and I don't really know why this happened, other than my own 'try to figure it out' guesses, you would think that vision would have had such an impact that my life might have evolved into something really big or special or I would become the once thought about missionary as my "looked-up-to and admired" uncle, right? Wrong! It would become like an impacted wisdom tooth while life went on. Until 10 years later, when it would be recalled. But in the meantime, life still happened!

At the age of 22 years, I finally decided I really wanted to move to Hawaii and did so in 1965. A year later, I realize my dream of Stewardess for United Airlines (now called Flight Attendants) and was based at JFK after the 5½ week training that took place in Chicago. I would fly the long layovers and enjoy every moment of my short-lived career. I was even chosen to fly the Nixon Presidential Campaign which lasted for several months.

My newfound career also allowed me to meet my future husband, who was a Steward for United Airlines, who was based in Hawaii and on a layover in San Francisco. I was very taken with him, and the feelings were mutual. It was pretty much love at first sight for us both. (Interestingly, while I was flying for the Nixon Campaign, he was chosen to fly the Agnew Campaign.)

In 1968, after six months of long-distance phone calls, constant phone calls and occasional meetings on a layover, he asked me to marry him. His proposal was absolutely classic. He slipped a ring on my finger, and then he announced, "I want you to marry me, but before you answer, I want you to know I'm married, but separated, and I have three children!" Holy smokes, was that a red flag or what? You're probably asking, "What were you thinking?" And to be honest, I obviously wasn't, or I just didn't care!

We had to wait the six months because children were involved in his divorce, and then we tied the knot— when I was seven months pregnant! Another classic move. He was not a believer in the Lord, but knew who He was, and wasn't attending a church. I knew Jesus but didn't have a personal relationship with Him until 1972.

I wish I could have seen the red flags, but when you think you are in love, you are just plain blinded, color blinded! I have five, not perfect, but accomplished children… two I gave birth to, yet I raised them all as "one." I never wanted any of this "step" or "half" in our family, and I worked tirelessly to keep them as one family.

"You have seen me tossing and turning through the night.
You have collected all my tears and preserved them in your
bottle! You have recorded every one in your book."
Psalm 56:8

Chapter 2

Shattered Dreams

"I can't do this anymore," I whispered in sorrowful surrender. Consumed with questions and desperately looking for answers while living with unbearable heartache, I realized the bondage I had been living in for so long had not only shattered all my dreams of a successful happy marriage but was also leaving me completely drained and empty.

Soon I became aware that the physical effects of my unhappiness were increasingly causing my body to break down due to all the stress that seemed to wrap me in its grip. Then, the enormous amounts of tears that were shed throughout all those years could have been measured in the gallons. And with that... my story begins.

As little girls, most of us have dreamt of that special day when we would walk down the aisle in our Cinderella designer gown, or the memory filled old taffeta and lace hand-me-downs from our mom or our grandmother's wedding day. The room would be filled with beautiful flowers, smiling faces, nodding heads with tears flowing down their cheeks; all the essence needed to present the magical long-awaited moment.

As the Fairy Princess or elegantly dressed lady gracefully steps forward, she is magnetically drawn to her handsome Prince in shining armor who is anxiously awaiting his partner, his supposed soul mate, the other half of himself, and her heart skips continuous beats in excitement and anticipation. Their vows are nervously but so eloquently spoken. Then finally an "I do" is whispered so affectionately, as if it were a prayer that beckoned a great "Amen" to seal it. All so beautiful and dreamy, the whole thought process. The plans for the perfect future that leaves no room for anything other than the "happily ever after."

Then one day the unimaginable... the unspeakable appears. A monster of a nightmare, that leaves you numb with shock and disbelief. A nightmare that, for many women and, believe it or not, some men, appears from nowhere, and the "I do" shockingly becomes "I can't. I just can't do this any longer." That's right, men too!

Where did this come from and how did it happen? For me personally, I didn't even see it coming. Why didn't I see it coming? But wait a minute. God put this marriage together, didn't He? Or did He?

Before I go any further, I want to be very honest in saying that the beliefs interjected along with my own experiences are purely mine. As for the experiences that have been shared with me by people I have known, and others of whom I had connected with during a conversation or had a chance meeting with one day, they are just that, someone else's of whom no names will be given. Combined, these various experiences speak volumes in similarities. They also speak of God's Will needing to take charge in our lives, especially the work He is doing right now as we all cry out to Him for help.

Jesus is the only one who can see clearly, and we need to keep our eyes upon Him, allowing His Will to be done. I have experienced a lot in my lifetime, in my faith walk, as I am sure many have, and I know my Lord's hand has been upon it all. I may not always see His hand or know what He is doing at a particular moment or while going through a particular trial, but I know beyond a shadow of doubt that He is in the midst of it all— going before me, guiding me and walking beside me, holding my hand.

Even in times when desperation would lead me to scream out "Lord, where are you? Do you see what's going on? What am I supposed to do and when do I do it? Where are You? Then, with a sigh of peaceful relief, He shows me He has it all under control, and He isn't about to let go of my hand.

I began thinking a lot about the incredible hurts and unbelievable heartache I had experienced in my wreck of a marriage, which led to writing thoughts down on paper, as I mentioned before. My intention was not to make sure I remembered each one as if to hold "him" accountable to the end, or to make it all indelible upon my brain so that I would never or could never forget what happened. Rather it was therapy. Therapy in facing it all; facing it and calling it by name or title or just voicing it for what it was.

Sometimes we try to push it all aside and pretend it never happened. Or we may throw a blanket over our heads and stick our fingers in our ears and sing "La, La, La, La, La!" Sometimes we are completely embarrassed or ashamed to admit we failed at such an important milestone as a four-decade marriage. Then before I knew it, my thoughts were turning into a testimony, not only to help my listening ears, but to possibly share with someone that may have gone through or is going through the same turmoil in their life.

There's a wonderful scripture I often turn to for encouragement because it never fails to soothe my frightened heart. It's from Isaiah 41:10, *"Fear not, for I am with you; Be not dismayed, for I am your God. I will strengthen you, Yes, I will help you, I will uphold you with My righteous right hand."*

With my constant cries "Dear God... dear God," He heard those cries and did something about it. You see, Jesus had been collecting all my tears and was putting them in a bottle... for a very long time.

One day, while considering Psalm 56:8, *"You number my*

wanderings; *Put tears into Your bottle; Are they not in Your book?"* And why it was important enough to be put in the Bible, I asked Him what He planned to do with that bottle. He told me He had put my name on it and would one day anoint me with those tears because they were so precious to Him.

I realized that every time a tear dropped, He caught it, just like He catches all your tears and is putting them in a bottle with your name on it. He also showed me He was not only with me at this very moment, but He had been with me every step of the way all through the years. He watched the whole me, the person God had planned for me to be, being formed Psalms 139:15-16, *"You were there while I was being formed in utter seclusion! You saw me before I was born and scheduled each day of my life before I began to breathe. Every day was recorded in your Book."*

I feel this scripture reveals such a personal and loving attentiveness of our Lord. He had been there, not just in happy times or difficult or indecisive times, but every moment I had hurt.

As I gained strength to face all that I had gone through, I soon felt a driving force to write my story and, Lord willing, it would one day be told. Reading Psalm 45:1 from TLB seemed to get my attention when I read, *"For I am as full of words as the speediest writer pouring out his story."*

Then one day, I picked up my NKJV Bible and read Psalm 45:1, and that same scripture jumped off the pages, *"My heart is overflowing with a good theme; I recite my composition concerning the King; my tongue is the pen of a ready writer"* and that was confirmation enough for me to begin.

Whether it was read or shared, it needed to be voiced. As I began to search the scriptures and focus on His word daily, I realized spiritual food is far more important than taking care of the many needs I projected as absolutely essential. I knew I couldn't grow in the knowledge of my Lord; much less fight the enemy without putting on all of God's armor and standing firmly on His word.

Ephesians 6:15-17 says, *"Wear shoes that are able to speed you on as you preach the Good News of peace with God. In every battle you will need faith as your shield to stop the fiery arrows aimed at you by Satan. And you will need the helmet of salvation and the sword of the Spirit – which is the Word of God."*

As I continued to write, the pages seemed to mount in number. I found myself pouring out page upon page of experiences I had gone through, as well as the many lessons learned along the way. Then, to my surprise, the ability to face my realities allowed my self-esteem and confidence to slowly immerge from a graveyard of ground-up dust to being able to stand up tall, without the "too many" years of mentally oppressed slouching.

Now I am beginning to feel three feet taller (my sister seems to delight in reminding me, "You're standing up much straighter now"). And too, I began to feel an overwhelming strength in positive acceptance of myself, knowing that although I didn't understand it all or even a little bit of what was happening, one thing I was sure of and that was Jesus was watching over me… He was walking beside me holding onto my hand.

But in the beginning, when my blinders were on and my heart was stubbornly determined to carry this heavy load of grief and destruction, I had no idea how much I would need His strength.

Shattered Dreams

"For he who sows to his flesh will of the flesh reap corruption,
but he who sows to the Spirit will of the Spirit
reap everlasting life.."
Galatians 6:8

Chapter 3

Oh! To Be a Fly on the Wall

It seems that in today's world, more so now than at any other time, a lot of unresolved issues are being brought to the wedding chapel anticipating a new life; an escape into a better new beginning, burying those issues and pretending they are no longer in their backpack. It looks as though there are a lot of excess pieces of "baggage" being set up and poised for target practice. It would seem quite unconscionable not to want to question what is going on.

I mean, everyone has problems, concerns, or difficulties they carry into the marriage, but the things I have noticed, and experienced firsthand, are just aiming for a breakdown, before the marriage has had a chance to get off on the right foot. Issues such as trust, forgiveness, not to mention possessiveness, jealousy, anger, control, and unhealthy sexual desires, all have the potential to destroy and eventually will, and the laundry list goes on and on. A lot of these issues are the hurtful things that were never dealt with or resolved in the early years because someone (or many someone's) did not care enough or love enough to pay attention to correcting or attempt to address the ill-fated direction that was being taken; a direction that would one day lead straight onto a destructive path.

Once the behaviors are allowed to be carried into the marriage, trouble eventually finds its way into the middle, aimed toward a split in that marriage union. The blame, resulting from these issues, can soon fester and quickly be displaced to the other spouse, and then it is only a matter of time before the unsuspecting spouse ends up being the punching bag for it all and wondering, as I always did, "where did that come from?" When blame is placed onto the other spouse, he or she ends up taking the rap for the deep rage that may have been suppressed for a long time, but continued to fester, sometimes since childhood. I know this to be true because I have seen it over and over again.

As a retired nurse, I have seen it in the clinics, the hospital, and I have been told horror stories from friends, even people that I did not know personally but somehow felt safe in confiding in me, about the horrible, ugly and unsuspecting trenches they have gone through with this sort of behavior and how they found themselves beaten down, whether physically, emotionally or broken by anger, jealousy and mistrust, which eventually zeroes in on spiritual brokenness. I can also attest to this truth in my own life. Believe me, anger and rage just plain does you in, wipes you out and breaks you down like nothing else can. Oh, my dear Lord, help us lay our excess baggage at Your feet and take hold of Your always extended hand, in willingness and acceptance of surrendering our hearts to the circumcision of Your loving Will.

I went through bouts of abuse with my husband for decades, and far too many to count—some verbal, others extremely emotional, too many were physical and often even spiritual. Sadly, like most wives who have had to endure the horrors of any type of abuse, it will never be easy to forget.

There are times even today that I can still feel his hands around my neck, holding me down on the bed until I would begin choking and gasping for breath. Then, for nothing better to do, he would stomp on my foot leaving me with painful neuropathy to this day.

He also used a gun to try to scare me too. Though he never pointed it at me, he was always threatening that he'd blow my head off or if I ever left him, he'd kill me. He liked to hold the gun and point it at anything or wave it around as if taunting and flaunting his seriousness in doing what he said he would. It's like he had to prove he meant what he said. It was always threatening and then blowing up. Then, after something was broken, he'd say, "Now look what you made me do." He'd blow up and then destroy something just to show me he could do what he wanted. This is often referred to the Honeymoon Stage: The blowing up, then destruction, then the apology, "I'll never do it again…" Until next time.

This one day he was just angry about something, I don't remember what… I never really knew what. But that day we were in the bedroom, and he had the gun in his hand, waving it around as he was swearing and telling me off, trying to scare me, of which he absolutely did, and he pointed it at the ceiling and shot. It was that evil look on his face, so angry and just wanting to pull the trigger, but he always stopped short, except that day.

As I am writing this, I can still see his face. He looked like he was about to explode before he pointed the gun down and shot the floor. Then he pointed it up at the ceiling and shot. My daughters were in their bathroom adjacent to our bedroom, just on the other side of our room. The gunshot is heard as my youngest gets out of the shower. My oldest pushes her down on the floor and drops on top of her. That bullet went through at an angle and hit just above the big mirror they would have been standing in front of had they not dropped to the floor.

The hole the bullet left in the wall was big and so easily seen. It was also a very painful reminder of that night none of us would ever forget. And then, to hear my ten-year-old daughter say, "Mommy, is Daddy going to kill us tonight?" was just another unbearable reminder of what my life had become.

My heart aches for all the children that have to experience and pay for what their parents did to them, and there are so many… mine included. My husband's anger also triggered many attacks on doors, walls, furniture, silverware, dishes, car windshield, and on and on, which were broken, bent, thrown, or destroyed. And most of the time, I would silently ask that same question, "Why? Where did that come from?"

Soon, you find yourself living in fear. Fear of saying the wrong thing; fear of saying the right thing, but at the wrong time, fear of being told, no matter how you have responded to a question, "You didn't answer the question", which silently announces, "You are in trouble now!" Or there is the fear of using a certain tone when asking, "What are you talking about?" Fear of wanting to visit children or grandchildren, or just go to lunch with a friend because there would be suspicions and questions of who will be there and what you talked about.

Then, you make sure you got home at the specific time, knowing that if you arrive even five minutes late, a finger would be tapping on the face of his watch, as your car slowing and almost cowardly drives in and parks. Fear that you are doing something wrong by "abandoning" him by babysitting grandchildren once a month, when that is the only time you get to see them.

You realize that you begin to use the fear to protect yourself while walking delicately upon eggshells because if you don't, the slightest thing will trigger an explosion that sets the rage firing in all directions. Just a word or glance or response, or a phone call at an inopportune moment; just a tiny piece of eggshell is all that is needed to set the whole keg of dynamite off. And then, the next day, the apologies would sound so sincere, and you forgive and just let it go. You let it go until the next time, even though it was promised never to happen again and again and again.

This brings to mind when a friend once commented, "Gee, you folks are always together. You must really be happy to spend so much time together." My smilingly sarcastic answer was, "Oh, it's just an eternal honeymoon!" You become the good little wife that is supposed to be submissive, no matter what, because you have been conditioned to his ownership. In fact, he mockingly often would say to me, "God gave you to me!" As if I were his possession to do with whatever he wanted.

I started to feel like I was deep within a pit of being used and controlled. I used to tell myself, "Well, if I have to be a doormat, I will be a doormat for Jesus." Of course, now I know that was an absolutely absurd and ridiculous statement to make. Jesus would never ever expect me or you or anyone else to be a so-called "Doormat" for Him. That is not what submission is!

Many years ago, my husband and I attended a graduation party with other company friends and acquaintances. It was quite enjoyable to be able to meet up with wives who I had not seen very often, some for years, while all the men were off to one side of the pavilion, enjoying themselves joking, laughing, and sharing their little stories of whatever, we women sat at a table, some distance from the men, and shared as well.

We all seem to like our little private space to share all that has gone on in our lives over the years. The children and how they've grown and all the sports they participated in and accomplishments they have attained. You know the usual? But then there seemed to be a very slow willingness amongst a few of us to share a little deeper; a little more personal. Smiles and pleasantries slowly became sobering for some of us.

I'm not sure how it all began, but someone mentioned something; a little hint of strain within her marriage, and then another would concur and before I knew it, I was hearing my story all over again. Oh, my dear goodness! Another least expected couple, one after another, mirror imaging my marriage and almost to a perfect replication.

My heart cried and became so heavy. I remember one of them who seemed to wear that same cellophane mask that I wore all the time; that same mask that announced, "Everything's okay in my life; my marriage is an eternal honeymoon." That mask seemed to shine like a neon sign pointing to deep concern and timid fear. I asked her if she would like to meet for coffee or lunch sometime. She slowly shook her head, with obvious concern in her eyes and told me, "That just would not be possible; it couldn't happen."

Well, stupid me, now what was I thinking? She gave me her phone number, of which I still have, some 20 or so years later, but have not had the courage to call. I often think of her and would really like to call and see how she's doing, but I remember her eyes being so cautious that now I am reluctant to do so. Besides, her husband was a very good friend of my husband... well, we know how far that would fly! (Update! I just spoke with a friend who mentioned that she runs into this gal every once in a while, so I did ask my friend to tell her I said hello.) Lord willing, we shall see where this leads, because I would really like to find out how she is holding up and be able to share all that the Lord has done for me.

Explosive anger can be frightening enough, but nothing can be worse than when it turns into rage. That is when the anger becomes so uncontrolled that the angry spouse just plain loses it! Words... ungodly, filthy, and unforgettable words, fly at highest frequency and with no respect to any human life or feelings, or care of being heard from afar. This is when the abused takes the rap, like I did for so long! Usually, the spouse is either in the way of the attack or they become the one purposely attacked. It can even be a stranger that takes the rap for all that rage.

I remember many a time when someone in another car had pulled out in front of our car or had driven a little too close for comfort. The next moment would become my worst nightmare of a fright flight! Suddenly, our car would become the bat out of a deep pit, chasing that other car just to teach the driver a lesson. Many times, I truly thought our car, with a Christian bumper sticker on it, was on a mission of vengeance with me holding on for dear life, "panic praying" all the while, following the culprit in the other car that had dared to do such a stupid thing as come within a mile's radius of our car. We would follow that car to its resting place, no matter where it went, or how long it took to get there.

It didn't matter whether it was a teenager or uniformed service man or just someone that had no idea of what they had done to make this maniac so angry. Suddenly, they would find their car forced to the side of the road or unwillingly parked in a driveway, then being pulled out of their car, and pushed or writhingly thrown against their car. I braved it many times, mentioning, "You know, that someone may have a gun and he may shoot you." But there was always a sarcastic or defiant banter back, "If I go down, I'll go down fighting and I won't go alone."

What unbelievable, arrogant, confidence mixed with rage of steel! That rage seemed to go out of its way to prove its power for some reason, almost like a craving for vengeance. Makes me think about the time when my windshield took a punch from a steel-like fist, causing it to shatter. Of course, I was reminded, "Now look what you made me do." That is what I was always told whenever there was an explosion. I was the cause of it all!

I have heard this over and over again from other women that claim being told the same thing. Like I've said, it doesn't take much to turn anger into rage. Just try swatting at a big, healthy yellow jacket's nest with a paper towel and see what happens!

Control Defined: According to Webster's dictionary: To have power over; to exercise restraining or directing influence over.

Control, what a powerful weapon and what devastating destruction when used for the wrong reasons! One spouse will project power over the other and expect him or her to do exactly as they dictate and do so according to explicit instructions and if they don't, they are in deep, deep, deep! I describe it as being on your spouse's time clock or watch. Everything is done according to his will and if it isn't, you are in big trouble and will suffer severe consequences. Better put, it is called control, and fear is one of the weaknesses that will hand over the reins and pave the way for that control.

This control thing has become such a problem in so many relationships today, resulting in countless women, and men in some cases, being subjected to physical, verbal, emotional and sexual abuse, which eventually leads to indescribable degradation and low self-esteem.

Once fear has taken control of her, she learns to cope with it by keeping the peace at all costs, which only leads to greater fear of what will happen if she does not succumb to the control that has entrapped her. Then it is just a matter of time before she has lost her self-identity, self-worth, and all integrity. Then to top it off, she sacrifices her knowledge of what is right before God, to desperately keep the peace. All her valued qualities vanish—just plain vanish!

Another friend from work once confided, "I think I married my dad." She told me her dad had always been an extremely angry, controlling man that would expect her, in so many words, to ask, "How high?" when he dictated, "Jump!"

She said when she was young, she lived in fear of his belt that had a huge, door knocker of a buckle on the end of it, because that was what he used to disciple her and her siblings with. Other times, he would wildly swing it in any direction, just to reinforce his position in control, hitting and knocking down or breaking anything in its way. Then, unbelievably, she ended up allowing herself to marry a man that would use similar control tactics upon her. She shared that when it finally dawned on her that she had allowed this to happen, she went from total disbelief to denial, and then to complete confusion as to what to do about it. I lost contact with her, so I am not sure how everything worked out for her, or if it ever did.

Another example of how behaviors are learned in our growing up years. For the abused or controlled, you learn to keep the peace no matter what. I learned very quickly that this "keeping the peace at all costs" is what I had to do to make sure I would not get into trouble. I learned to keep peace for my children as well, so they would not get into worse trouble or, if they did, I would step in and take on the trouble for them, just to save them.

You quickly realize your life is spent going in circles within an entrapment and there doesn't seem to be anything that can be done to escape from it or make it all better. Then, if you do make a move to step out of the set boundaries, you can almost bet it will only be a matter of time before something is broken, damaged or destroyed.

Fortunately, because of work schedules, there were many times when the children and I were blessed to enjoy the freedom of going to the beach or to the mall, or the movies. And sometimes we would stay up late at night, make popcorn, and play a game or watch TV. Just fun, together times without being told we couldn't and without overbearing relentless control. We could breathe peacefully and just enjoy one another. There seemed an unspoken permission to be normal; permission to be ourselves and not have to be cautious or fearful. Those times became so precious, and we welcomed them as we looked forward to the next with anticipation. My daughter recently mentioned how peaceful those times were when he was gone.

My heart breaks when I hear children, especially after they have grown into adults, confess that they didn't have fond memories of their father or mother, during their growing up years. How tragic it is to miss so much togetherness. I find it interesting how a father or mother would strive for family to be together, doing everything together, and then manage to push everyone away; everyone who had ever wanted to love them.

Sadly, some people just don't get it! I honestly believe some men are truly convinced that control over their spouse and family is their guarantee that their loved ones will forever be his and they will never leave him. That's why he always, always threatened to kill me if I left.

I also believe that, because of some kind of traumatic experience in the growing up years, there may often be a spirit of abandonment that has presented itself and just will not release the abusive spouse. This fear of abandonment will cement an unhealthy relationship for the whole family. Children are the ones we try to protect, but because of inability to do so safely, they end up holding onto horrible memories; memories that couldn't have been prevented under these circumstances. In time, those children, like mine, will suppress those memories and just move on as if nothing ever happened or try to convince themselves those times have been forgotten.

However, the day will come when somehow those memories will resurface and open the flood gates, bringing up all kinds of thoughts; thoughts of anger, rage (all over again) and questions that will demand answers and then answers that may want to seek revenge instead of forgiveness.

I know my children have expressed their feelings about their memories growing up in our home and the questions they are now being faced with because of those years. Uncomfortable memories will reluctantly be forced to resurface reminding them of the pain, anger, and resentment they had felt through the years, along with other thoughts they had buried.

The only good thing that can come out of all this is the fact that children will be faced with their need to express their feelings and be able to release them, hopefully to the Lord. With prayer and encouragement, they will see the need to confront those feelings with a genuine way to forgive their father or mother.

I have learned this is the only way to truly find any peace in my heart and mind, and I encourage my children every chance I get to think about forgiveness. Matthew 6:14-15, Jesus said, *"For if you forgive men their trespasses, your heavenly Father will also for give you. But if you do not forgive men their trespasses, neither will your Father forgive your trespasses."*

Forgiving is the only way to release someone that has hurt you into God's hands so He can work in them. A person, whether grown or child cannot bury these memories in their subconscious and pretend it is all gone and never happened. It will one day eat you up if this issue of suppression is not faced and addressed.

One of my children told me once that she felt I was a good mentor when it came to teaching the rights and wrongs that should be learned in life and how I had taught them all about the love of God, but was very sad to see the way I had always "wimped" out, as she called it, when it came to allowing myself to be treated the way I had always been. That just about broke my heart to hear that said, because I absolutely loved being a mom and I loved my children and I tried so hard to be an example of strength. I guess how we see ourselves isn't always how others see us.

My desire as a mother was to teach and guide my children, my gifts from God, how to live a good life that would be honorable and blessed, and make sure they knew God's word and His great love for them. I felt this was my duty and I truly thought I had done a pretty fair job of it. But to hear that exposed truth from her really did open my eyes and cause me to realize my reality was being transferred to my children. Unfortunately, it didn't stop the mistreatment that I continued to allow myself to take.

Wow! Of course, now she understands it was because of the fear I had for his temper and the rage that so often blew like a blowtorch. She was being forced to remember all the things she wanted to forget. I honestly filled up more of that bottle of tears, that's for sure. I just hope Jesus had planned for something a lot bigger than a multi-gallon receptacle. I am sure He did!

I believe and would like to think most people do as well, that family is such an important part of our lives, or at least it should be. I truly feel this makes God happy, because if it wasn't for Him in the first place, we would not have a family entity.

Of course, I'm sure there are many who would like to comment on that certain family member who must have been placed "out of place" within their family! Just being blessed with family; with children and grandchildren, sprinkled with friends who love and appreciate being included is such a normal, memory making part of everyone's life, is how it should be.

Those times spent together are wonderful and pleasurable and should not be used for guilt because you enjoyed those times. I remember planning to join my co-workers for a special luncheon, but at the last minute, because my husband decided he wanted to be a part of those plans too, I chose not to attend. I would have been terribly uncomfortable having him there, especially when it made no sense. He later told me, "Good you cancelled because you didn't even ask my permission to go in the first place."

I was supposed to have lunch with five other ladies from work who were getting together to bid goodbye to one of our coworkers who was leaving the company. I just couldn't imagine eating and conversing "girl talk" or "little nothings" to one another with him present, when he would be the only male there and did not know any of my co-workers. Of course, my friends told me later that it would be fine if he wanted to attend, but I was feeling sick to my stomach just thinking about that get together.

Visiting my family was another important and anticipated time for me because we all lived great distances from one another and rarely ever got to see each other. Just traveling anywhere was a big conflict of interest because he never wanted to go and if he didn't go, I would be expected not to go, as well. I was always told, "Not now" or "It's not the right time" or "It's not safe."

After so many years of disappointment of not being able to travel to see family, my dad finally told me later, he had always thought maybe I didn't want to see him and my mom, or the rest of my family for that matter. That really crushed me, to think my dad thought that.

Mind you, I was never ever told I could not go anywhere or visit with anyone. Rather, it was the anticipated sarcastic remarks; the vile comments of "you care more about them than you do for me" that made it clear that I had better beware of what I wanted or what I did. Or there were the unspoken words that if I ever made a decision, that I already knew in my heart was a red flag being waved in front of an intimidating rage, I was in serious trouble.

You see, for a lot of spouses, control is not always spoken clearly, nor is it spoken audibly; it isn't clear cut at all. Does that make sense? It's the look you get; the underlying body projection and demeanor or the curt, rude, and sarcastic comments that blast in your ears of what is permissive and what is definitely not. It's the silent words that slam doors or the objects that lay in waiting that soon take flight in unspecified directions and you pray it won't be in yours. You never know what is going to be broken or destroyed.

Like the saying goes, "actions speak louder than words"! In my case, after so many years of this type of coping, I realized I was living a lie. I truly believe he knew the unhealthy control he used over me, and I think that is why he constantly, often demandingly, wanted to hear me say I loved him. And every time I did say it, it seemed to grate across my heart and my conscience because, after so many years of mistreatment, it had finally become a lie.

It was so difficult to keep tolerating an empty, fearful, and controlled life, but I did because I couldn't handle the rage and anger that resulted if I didn't. Then, to top it all off and seal my fate, there were the frequent threats on my life if I didn't like the way we were living or if I ever dared to entertain the thought of leaving him. In other words, I had to learn to tolerate my doom.

Again, I would say, "If I have to be a doormat, I will be one for Jesus!" But, as I said before, that was just absurd. That thought is a bold-faced lie from the enemy. Halleluiah! I am not a doormat, and neither are you and I will never consider that thought ever again.

My married life held so much unhappiness that my nights became my oasis over too many years; my inner room where no one could enter as I silently cried myself to sleep begging God to please help me. There were times, I will admit, when I would question what I had gotten myself into, by marrying someone so angry, so controlling, but then I would think of my beautiful children and quickly ask God's forgiveness for even considering that my whole marriage had been a huge mistake.

I had to remember that this was the choice I made, and I truly thought I loved him. Then again, I question whether I was truly ready to take on the responsibility of marriage or if I only loved the idea of being married. Who knows at this point? But I realize now, I didn't take my decision to marry before the Lord. In fact, I really didn't think I needed to ask the Lord what He thought, as I wasn't living a God-surrendered life at that time.

Three years later, though, I would have a surrendered, fall in love with my Lord and Savior Jesus Christ experience. The sad part is that I had no idea of the extent of his temper before we had married. In fact, I did not take the time to really get to know him or how he would react to any given situation. I didn't know about his jealousies, temperament, possessiveness, or his strong sexual urges that just seemed wrong and unnatural.

Believe me, this is no way to live. It's not healthy and it's definitely not glorifying to the Lord. Control, used in every one of these dysfunctions, will eventually rob and cripple a spouse. It will deteriorate the self-worth, confidence, and identity, eventually manipulating all reasoning and ability to cope. Then, brokenness will leave you with a feeling of total inadequacy, covered in a blanket of guilt that is so hard to describe.

These feelings begin to paralyze you until you feel like you have been doomed and there is no way to escape from it. I know I am not the only person who has gone through this, and I know for sure, there are too many bound to the fallacy of what is supposed to be a "normal" marriage, such as this.

One of my dear friends once shared how she went through an awful scary moment when she decided to leave her abusive husband. During a raging assault upon her, he held her captive with a gun pointed at her head and threatened to pull the trigger. Fortunately, her sister-in-law, who knew of their troubled marriage, seemed to have an eerie feeling that something was wrong and, having a key to their house, barged in at the perfect moment and charged between the two of them. Standing in front of my friend, throwing her arms back around her to protect her, she told her brother to go ahead and shoot, but he would have to shoot her first. He was so distraught; he threw his gun to the floor and ran out of the house. The two of them grabbed what things they could and left as quickly as possible, afraid he might have second thoughts and return.

Like I have said before, rage and anger can become like wildfire and when lit, the damage can be staggering. It is truly heartbreaking, and my prayer is that these out-of-control spouses will be able to find help or refuge of some kind before that rage explodes into permanent harm.

Do you think the Lord is just a little disturbed by this? Do you really think He is looking the other way? You better believe the answers are "Yes" to the first question and definitely "No" to the second.

""I have heard your prayer, I have seen your tears;
surely I will heal you."
2 Kings 20:5

Chapter 4

Broken Vows, Broken Promises

Infidelity is incredibly devastating and can leave an indelible scar that tests one's ability to ever trust again. It questions faith in the spouse who has cheated, for a long time and often for the rest of the marriage, unless the cheated one decides to forego the forgiving and "looking the other way" and chooses to get out of the marriage, of which the Bible does speak about. Matthew 5:32, Jesus said, *"But I say to you that whoever divorces his wife for any reason except sexual immorality causes her to commit adultery; and whoever marries a woman who is divorced commits adultery."*

I believe the Bible does give divorce the okay in the case of adultery, but I also believe if at all possible and if the couple truly wants to try and heal their marriage, there should be a striving for reconciliation with a willingness to forgive and work to resolve the problems and issues that might have had a hand in the adulterous act. Again, we see how the husband and wife must work with one another and pray and seek the Lord's hand upon their marriage. It is not an easy thing to do, forgiving your spouse for taking another to his bed. When I found out my husband had been unfaithful to our vows, it was the most difficult thing I would have to endure.

I eventually forgave him, but it wasn't until quite a while after he had first confessed it to me. I truly wrestled with his admission of adultery and the fact that I needed to forgive him, and I did wrestle with it for many months after that.

A gazillion of thoughts go through your mind when you are found in this situation. Was I not enough? Did he stop loving me? Did he love her? I would ask myself repeatedly what I did to allow this to happen. But wait a minute, I was always there for him, and I never denied him of myself or of anything else, for that matter. Was he fizzling out? Again, I would take the blame for his action. What about the children? Do I leave him? But he said he was sorry; do I leave him anyway? Can I ever trust him again? How do I live with him or be intimate again without this becoming a black veil between us?

Tons of questions shouted in my ears on a daily basis, and I found myself feeling betrayed and consumed with disbelief and soon falling headfirst into total depression. Then one day the Lord spoke to me and began to tenderly ask me questions of how I was feeling about all that I was going through. He asked, "Do you feel cheated?" I said, "Yes." He then said, "I did too, first." He asked, "Do you feel you were lied to?" I said, "Yes." He said, "I was too, first." He asked, "Do you feel you were betrayed?" Again, I said, "Yes." He said, "I was too, first." He kept asking if I was feeling all of these different emotions and every time I said yes, He said He went through it first. He was letting me know that He knew exactly how I felt and because He had experienced those feelings first, He would help me get through it if I would let Him.

Jesus told me there were only two things I could do. One, I could remain angry and depressed and be miserable the rest of my life and even leave my husband because I had every right to do so. Or I could forgive my husband and give it all to Him (Jesus); to trust Jesus to help me. Well, the latter is what I chose, but mainly "because of the children."

They were young and I couldn't bear breaking up the so called "security" of their home. Good heavens, just listen to me! How self-sacrificing can one become? I wanted and needed the Lord's help because of the children, while at the same time I feared what my husband always threatened, that he would "blow" me away if I ever took his kids away or even thought about leaving him. Wow, there's that fear again, big time!

What a ridiculous paradox and to tell you the truth, that was not trusting God at all. I may have stepped in that direction, but I did not let go of the fear that was held in the control of my husband. I may not have handed it all over to the Lord at that time, but I did verbalize forgiveness to my husband. And I desperately tried to work at our marriage to keep it together. Like I said, it was the most difficult thing I have ever done.

I do confess, all the forgiveness and working toward a better marriage did not make it like brand new again, but I gave it my best because marriage was supposed to be for keeps and it was for the sake of my children. In reality, I believe the betrayed carry the scars silently for the rest of their lives.

Yes, there is available healing when the Lord is sought and given the surrendered pain that we seem to hold on to. But sometimes, we want to hold on to that pain as a personal badge of brokenness, unwilling to turn loose of it even though we know we should.

Betrayal is often silent because many bury it and won't let on. Some will admit to their situation if they feel safe and secure enough to open up and face it with someone, but many will hide it. Sadly, the scars of betrayal can become so deep that it is difficult to see beyond the pain, disbelief, and discouragement while carrying the failure.

Then, if there has been a split in the marriage and divorce has resulted, it becomes difficult to even think of new relationships, without those scares coming to surface again. That is when a whole new batch of issues develops. But, as I have said, it is a willingness to face those scars and look upon Jesus and His scars!

Many don't realize that the betrayal opens a door of healing; healing that lies in forgiving and eventually the willingness to show Agape love. He, our Lord Jesus, went through it first, and this changes everything—if we allow ourselves the courage to let go and let God! But, then again, I am aware that for some, the scars can leave a toughness that is so hard to penetrate or remove. For many, they just can't imagine letting go and experiencing the freedom that Jesus offers because their whole world is blockaded by painful scars; scars that do not and will not allow anyone else to get close.

I do know for sure that when the Lord makes all things new again, it is just that. Sadly, I hadn't learned that yet because it had not happened yet. But you still look to the Lord to help you do what you think is right. I cannot tell you how I filled that bottle of mine. You know, the one filled with tears, with my name on it!

*"I say then: Walk in the Spirit, and you shall
not fulfill the lust of the flesh."*
Galatians 5:16

Chapter 5

Ultimate Betrayal

Yes, adultery is a tough obstacle to overcome, but a lustful, sick, craze for sex; the unquenchable desire to play out fantasies, just like in porn movies, outside the privacy of God-given sexual intimacy is wrong. Fulfilling ungodly filthy acts, even spousal rape like I had to endure, instead of the normal and enjoyable sexual relationship between the husband and wife is beyond all comprehension.

God said sin is sin, but I cannot imagine anything being more harmful to a marriage than this one because it destroys, not only the trust and protected fidelity within marriage, but the beautiful bond of oneness I feel God had planned for us. And, if allowed to enter the sanctity of the marriage, it will tarnish the spiritual makeup of a spouse... both spouses, actually. It is a huge betrayal!

"You better try to enjoy this because this is what keeps marriages together" or "This is what makes a marriage stronger!" "This is what married couples have to do to keep their marriage alive; to keep it going." This is what I was told repeatedly, starting very early in our marriage. Again, I would ask God, "Where did this come from and why?"

If this is true, what my husband always says is okay in a "normal" marriage—in all marriages—then why do I feel so dirty? Why do I feel this unnatural sick craze has destroyed me; destroyed my desire to even want to experience what God had meant for our enjoyment through marriage? I do believe it has played a huge part in destroying my marriage, and like I said, I cried bitter tears for too many years because of it. I remember asking him, after I had left our marriage and was at safe distance from any physical backlash, why he felt the need to control what he was so freely given. He had no answer. Four years later, I am still unable to wrap my understanding around his actions.

Stepping back 46 years, why had I not seen that first red flag? That explosion of anger, the night before we were to be married, that blurted out of nowhere. Although it alerted me by getting my attention, I didn't know how to react. It kind of stunned me and although it kept me awake most of the night wondering where that temper had come from and what ignited the fuse, I guess I just pushed it out of my mind.

Honestly, the thought of tying the knot, so to speak, did enter my mind whether this was the right thing to do or not, but it was only a fleeting thought over a very short moment. Then, the next day arrives and we have just gotten married, celebrated with a fine dinner at an expensive restaurant on the beach, with our Best Man and Maid of Honor. It was meant to be a very special and joyous celebration, and when we had finished our beautiful dinner, it was announced that we were going to complete our special evening with a movie. A movie? Really?

I felt so happy about my wedding day, even though I was seven months pregnant, we made everything right by getting married—the beautiful dinner shared with our friends who stood up for us, and now I was sitting next to my prince in this movie theater, with these same friends… and watching a porn movie!

I was crushed to the core, as if my heart were exploding within my chest, feeling as if in a state of shock. I could not believe what my eyes were witnessing and suddenly I had a sick feeling in the pit of my stomach. All I could do was turn my head and try to avoid looking at the screen.

The movie seemed to last forever and all I remember was hearing my new husband and his friends giggling and making little comments. In fact, it got to the point that I really wanted to get up and leave or I was going to get really sick; I wanted to throw up. Dear God, dear God, what is happening? There's the second red flag, but now it is too late… we are already married! The helplessness was just astounding.

Today I question myself as to why I didn't just get up and walk out of that movie theater. But where would I walk? What could I do? I felt frozen from my neck down. My body just wouldn't move. I will never get the image out of my head. And worse, out of my heart!

1 Thessalonians 4:3-8, *"For God wants you to be holy and pure, and to keep clear of all sexual sin so that each of you will marry in holiness and honor-not in lustful passion as the heathen do, in their ignorance of God and his ways. And this also is God's will; that you never cheat in this matter by taking another man's wife, because the Lord will punish you terribly for this, as we have solemnly told you before. For God has not called us to be dirty minded and full of lust, but to be holy and clean. If anyone refuses to live by these rules, he is not disobeying the rules of men but of God who gives his Holy Spirit to you."*

This is God's word, but how differently we live today. It has become common place for one or the other spouse to commit adultery at some point in the marriage and society seems to brush it off. I have heard comments from friends and associates at work, "I'm not surprised". But why was it not a surprise?

Isn't it interesting how far we have come since God gave us His commands on adultery? Look at what the Bible says in Leviticus 20:10, *"If a man commits adultery with another man's wife, both the man and the woman shall be put to death."* Yet today, adultery is brushed off and doesn't seem to hold the same severity of consequences as God had said it should.

Am I saying we should "tar and feather" and bury 10 feet under, all who commit adultery? No, of course not. But I am saying that it is more important to think about the severity of breaking this command, God's command. We need to remember the beautiful bond between husband and wife that God intended, the wedding vows that were promised, and look at adultery as sin. Where is the honor and the respect?

Like I said earlier, you have to work at marriage every day and every new day, you start all over again. Why isn't it enough for a man to be satisfied with one woman? Of course, I truly believe we should try to be physically attractive to our spouses, but there is so much more that needs to be done in order for a marriage to stay healthy.

It does take a lot of work; working together, forgiveness, understanding, compassion, communication, spending time with each other, listening and being sincerely interested in one another, giving your all to each other, even if your 100 percent is only 60 and his is 90, or the other way around. We give our all as best we can.

There are a lot more things that keep a marriage fresh and new and together, but the head of the list has to be Jesus, because if He, like I have said before, is not first in the marriage, nothing is going to work or grow. The marriage has to be founded on His word and what glorifies Him, and I tell you right now, sexual sin is not what edifies each other, nor does it give satisfaction, physically, emotionally or spiritually. We continually have to work at it especially when the calendars are filled with responsibilities and work, and then trying to set a special day or evening for that quality time with each other.

I think women owe it to their husbands to be alluring in that special way that he enjoys, but only for him and certainly for his eyes only. I was made to believe (there's that learned fear held by control, again) that I had to be alluring to other men, so it would enhance our intimacy and allow him the enjoyment and satisfaction that he seemed to crave. I was told what to wear, what to do, and how to do it, in order for him to be satisfied. I will tell you right now, that is a lie from the pit of hell, and it will destroy the relationship between the husband and wife just as fast as a wildfire on a blistering hot summer day.

I believe it is quite normal for couples to find a need to keep their intimacy refreshed and try something different or new now and then, but most assuredly in agreement with one another and certainly not by inviting the enemy to waltz right in and destroy what you have, by living out fantasies in public view. It ruined mine and it not only destroyed the marriage, but it also caused me to realize that I no longer loved my husband. I lost all respect and trust for him.

I got to the point that I couldn't wait to go to bed at night; to be able to close my eyes so he couldn't enter my world or my space. That was my reprieve and I looked forward to that time. It would be as if I was gone by midnight, but still there in the morning.

I found, that living with the repercussions of his infidelity, not just once, and volatile control, the degradation he put me through, was all a huge betrayal. That is when I said I can't do this any longer, and when the moment presented itself, after years of pleading with God to release me, **I left.**

Men, you need to see the beauty in your wives and really appreciate who they are. They are supposed to be your gift from God. Your wives are not your play toy outside of the intimate privacy God gave you, so please treat her very respectfully and tenderly in this because God is surely watching.

Also know that He is watching every time you look at a porn movie, search the internet for sexual satisfaction, and allow untamed roaming eyes and tempted lips to hunt down gratification in places you would not want anyone to know you frequent. The enemy would have you believe, as I was told to believe, that this is all a part of the norm for marriage—it's what we all do and it's truly okay. But that is not only a lying trap, but it forces God to eventually deal with you in a way I am sure you will not enjoy.

The NKJV Bible says it so well in James 1:12-16, *"Blessed is the man who endures temptation; for when he has been approved, he will receive the crown of life which the Lord has promised to those who love Him. Let no one say when he is tempted, 'I am tempted by God'; for God cannot be tempted by evil nor does He Himself tempt anyone. But each one is tempted when he is drawn away by his own desires and enticed. Then, when desire has conceived, it gives birth to sin; and sin, when it is full grown brings forth death. Do not be deceived, my beloved brethren."*

Did you hear that? Sin brings forth death. Spiritual death can consume both spouses. I feel sexual abuse is undoubtedly one of the most horrendously ugly, harmful, and painful sins and it presents itself in many color-coated rationalized forms, and I found myself broken with embarrassment; shamed with hate and contempt for just considering the thought of making "our marriage a total success and keeping it alive" by performing to his desires. Keep it alive for whom? For him; for me? for us?

The vile disgust for all of these evil acts will cause bitterness and deep regret and if it is continued throughout the marriage, it will eventually change the way you look upon your husband, yourself and others. I am also quite puzzled and completely in disbelief at my husband's desire to dangle me before other men for his satisfaction and gratification, because he always had such a jealousy toward other men; fearful that another man would dare to look at me. It just doesn't make sense to me, and after more than four decades of living like this, I got tired of trying to figure it out.

Many people act as if they can get away with just about anything, especially within the boundaries of marriage. "What can it hurt, if she/he doesn't know?" "I won't tell if you don't." "It's okay, because everyone else is doing it, and besides, it will just make me love her even more." "It was just sex. It didn't mean anything at all." We need to stop fooling ourselves and realize that sin will eventually find us out and it will corrupt and corrode our marriages, our lives, our spiritual relationship with God like nothing else can. We need to see our spouses as more than just sex objects, too.

Men, stop using your wives as just "boy toys", if that is what you think is okay. It may bring you pleasure momentarily, but it ends up destroying your relationship with your wife, destroys your marriage, and absolutely does not edify the Lord. Sometimes I wonder, does anyone ever ask if these actions are okay with God? Do they break His heart? We need to realize this is just another facet of control, and the learned fear will always succumb to that control.

I once heard a pastor on the radio say, "Men, if you keep this up, treating your wives like you do, in an unworthy and ungodly way, she is one day going to leave, and you will never get her back!"

"...even so we also should walk in newness of life."
Romans 6:4

Chapter 6

And Two Are Supposed To Become One

My story encompasses what I believe God has to say about marriage and what I perceive He intended it to be. I know it must have been quite pleasing to God when He instituted marriage. However, I can't help but feel how saddened He must be to see how the privileges of marriage and the loving bond of oneness that He intended, has been misused and has become so (repeat) distorted that the "I do" sometimes becomes "I can't!" I can't do this any longer.

The encouragement and comfort that I have received from the scriptures throughout my faith walk have come from The Living Bible (TLB) and the New King James Version (NKJV). These two

Bibles of mine are so marked up with dates when the scriptures were given to me, along with underlining and highlighting, and covered with notes and scribbles. Dear Lord, I pray I never lose them! These are routes, taken on my life's road map that have guided me through it all. And since God is the one that created it all, I will start at the beginning.

I truly feel we need to be reminded of what He has ordained as a covenant, so I would like to take a look at what marriage is all about, the role that the husband and wife were meant to play, according to God's plan, and the dysfunction, disappointments and abuses of the marriage bond that are so prevalent in too many marriages today.

In Genesis 2:18 it says, And the Lord God said, *"It isn't good for man to be alone; I will make a companion for him, a helper suited to his needs."* After causing Adam to fall into a deep sleep, God proceeded to remove one of his ribs and made a woman, Eve. Therefore, the woman became part of man.

Mind you, God did not make woman out of Adams foot, so he could step on her, rather from Adam's rib so she is joined with him. Genesis 2:24, "This explains why a man leaves his father and mother and is joined to his wife in such a way that the two become one person." And again, Mark 10:7-9, *"For from the very first He made man and woman to be joined together permanently in marriage; therefore a man is to leave his father and mother, and he and his wife are united so that they are no longer two, but one. And no man may separate what God has joined together."*

We all know this fact, from reading God's word. We have read it countless times and even those of whom may say they don't believe in God or do not profess Jesus as Lord, have heard something about the Garden of Eden and what transpired. I'm sure there have even been jokes made around the many water coolers throughout the ages (I have heard a few myself, so I know they are out there!) about the fact that a man has one less rib than a woman because she was made from it. Or there is the distorted view of woman being created explicitly for man, for his use and to his service. (Hmm, that rings a bell!) This is not what God's word is saying!

What it is saying is that God did not intend for man to be alone. Man and woman needed a companion, a help mate so God instituted marriage and within that marriage they would hopefully produce children, becoming a family unit and follow His beautiful blueprint of such a special bond.

Then, there is one of many benefits stated by Ecclesiastes 4:9-12, *"Two can accomplish more than twice as much as one, for the results can be much better. If one falls, the other pulls him up; but if a man falls when he is alone, he's in trouble. Also, on a cold night, two under the same blanket gain warmth from each other, but how can one be warm alone? And one standing alone can be attacked and defeated, but two can stand back-to-back and conquer; three is even better, for a triple-braided cord is not easily broken."* (By the way, that triple braided cord; I like to view it as God, the third strand, holding the hands of man and woman.) Someone to love, share and communicate the "everything's and whatever's", to start a family and so on. Husband and wife work together, share together, help and care for one another and if blessed, would raise their children together. That, I believe, is the gift of marriage.

All through the Bible, we find scriptures that teach how we are to treat the union of marriage, but as we all have come to know, there is a huge problem in the world today and many marriages and families, even amongst Christians within our churches, are suffering spiritual harm and destruction. More simply put, too many marriages are falling apart, away from God's intention. God bless the marriages that have been able to weather the torrential storms and are still standing. I truly thought mine would be one of those rarities.

Now days, many couples desire to speak their own words in vowing their love to one another, but the basic wedding vows go something like this:

I, (name), take you (name), to be my (wife/husband), to have and to hold from this day forward, for better or for worse, for richer, for poorer, in sickness and in health, to love and to cherish; from this day forward until death do us part.

Or another version:

I, (name), take you, (name), to be my [opt: lawfully wedded] (husband/wife), my constant friend, my faithful partner and my love from this day forward. In the presence of God, our family and friends, I offer you my solemn vow to be your faithful partner in sickness and in health, in good times and in bad, and in joy as well as in sorrow. I promise to love you unconditionally, to support you in your goals, to honor and respect you, to laugh with you and cry with you, and to cherish you for as long as we both shall live.

These vows hold such deep meaning, as they should, if one truly listens to what they are promising and realize it is meant for both the husband and wife. Unfortunately, and very sadly, the meaning can lose its luster through the "better or for worse" years, as many can testify to especially when only one spouse is trying to keep those vows cleaned and polished. God created marriage and meant for it to be held sacred.

Marriage is a lot of work and there are constant ups and downs sprinkled with an incredible amount of learning, but it is to be enjoyable and fulfilling, but most of all sacred. For the man, there would never be another woman, and for the woman, there would never be another man, unless the "death do us part" is a factor for either spouse. The two would become one, forsaking all others. Period.

One of my beloved daughters once asked, "How do you have a perfect marriage?" My response to her was, "You don't. You have to work at it 26 hours a day, and when you wake up the next morning, you start all over again." She was struggling with the normal marriage growth spurts, so all I got from that answer to her question was a mouth dropped stare! You know the "you've got to be kidding me" kind of stare? Yes ma'am, you work at it endlessly. You also learn to pray constantly, and sometimes panic-praying works just fine, thank you very much!

Okay, you might be thinking, "And?" What's the point you are getting at and why do I sense a big fat BUT somewhere along the way! You are right. My married life was, in my eyes and in my heart, forever, no matter what. It's just that the WHAT is what wedged itself into the middle. It's the WHAT that betrayed, abused, and crushed a more than four-decade marriage and that's when I said, "I can't do this any longer."

Ephesians 5:21-33 talks about the role of the husband and wife and how they are to treat one another in marriage. *"Honor Christ by submitting to each other. You wives must submit to your husbands' leadership in the same way you submit to the Lord. For a husband is in charge of his wife in the same way Christ is in charge of his body the Church. He gave his very life to take care of it and be its Savior! So you wives must willingly obey your husbands' in everything, just as the Church obeys Christ. And you husbands, show the same kind of love to your wives as Christ showed to the Church when he died for her, to make her holy and clean, washed by baptism and God's Word; so that he could give her to himself as a glorious Church without a single spot or wrinkle or any other blemish, being holy and without a single fault. That is how husbands should treat their wives, loving them as part of themselves. For since a man and his wife are now one, a man is really doing himself a favor and loving himself when he loves his wife! No one hates his own body but lovingly cares for it, just as Christ cares for his body the Church, of which we are parts. So again I say, a man must love his wife as a part of himself; and the wife must see to it that she deeply respects her husband – obeying, praising and honoring him."*

As I read the word "obeying", I really had to ponder what God truly meant by that, especially in comparison to what was expected of me in my marriage. That is, what was expected from God verses what was expected from my husband. Obeying? Hmmm... Really, is that right? Okay, that must mean whatever the husband says, you do, right? No questions asked! If he says jump, you as the submissive wife is required to ask, "How high, honey?" No, I don't believe that is what the Bible teaches, and I don't feel that is what the Lord had in mind.

Now mind you, all that I have to say is purely my opinion, but I feel the whole kit and caboodle is pretty much on que. You can move the pieces around a bit, but the whole of the matter is what I want to talk about. I believe a husband is supposed to be the head of the house. However, there may be some instances where the wife needs to fulfill this role. At any rate, he is the protector, sole or joint provider, consoler, leader, listener, helper, and lover.

No one is perfect and this may be a tough bill to fill for some, but I feel if a wife feels she can look up to her husband and view him in this over all role, she will respect him and be willing to stand by him, submitting to his leadership, trusting, and believing he is taking care of his lady. After all, God blessed him with her. Did you notice that word "respect?" If the husband leads his wife in submission to the Lord's leading, with respect, there will be a flow of honor, submission, and trust in his leadership.

I want to interject something that I have become aware of,

and that is being submissive does not mean the wife has to be obedient to everything her husband asks of her. For instance, if he has directed or requested, she do something that she knows in her heart is not of God and it's not going to glorify God or be blessed by God, that is where she needs to speak up and question what he wants her to do. There definitely needs to be a discussion concerning the reasons for his request.

Of course, not all of us who share my situation may feel safe enough to stand up to those requests because it would be a great detriment to do so. I found myself in these situations too many times and because I feared the repercussions of doing or saying anything other than complying with obedience to his request; often times blatant order, all I could do was pray and hope. Hope that Jesus would intervene and stand by me knowing what was going on.

We all (women and men alike), want to feel appreciated and loved, knowing that we can trust and feel safe with one another because we know God has not only set this way up for us, but He is always watching over us in this union. It flows, or at least it is supposed to, if the husband and wife are truly seeking God's blessing in their marriage. Then again, there is going to be a disaster waiting around the corner of life, if self-centeredness and lack of care for the marriage bond is not respected and viewed as a blessing from God.

Do I believe God put all marriages together? No, I do not. God instituted marriage, but I do not believe He purposefully put all married couples together. Many make that decision for themselves, and if that decision or that couple has not sought the Lord's leading and blessing, it is in for trouble before the church bells have begun to ring! I believe many couples jump into marriage without thinking twice, without prayer, counseling and definitely without counting the cost of that commitment of responsibility and the committed work that is going to be involved, only to become disillusioned and dissatisfied.

Many marriages fall apart when the going gets rough. The work involved and the weight of the difficulties often times become too much for the couple to handle, especially if one partner ends up carrying the brunt of responsibility because the other doesn't care to see the importance of helping or contributing. There are many who marry for the sexual gratification, but when that alluring pheromone is gone or has become old and boring, they throw in the towel and either quit or allow the scent of another to capture their attention. Many have said or will say, "the spark is gone". It's like the carbonation has fizzled out. Really?

Many years ago, a friend I worked with was going through a very shaky relationship with her fiancé. She came to me and angrily shouted, "If I can't have him, I at least want his baby!" He was fizzling out and she wanted to make sure she kept a piece of him. Well, she had his baby alright, but ended up adopting the baby out to someone else, and he went into the service and never looked back. As far as I know, the two never got back together. What a pitiful excuse and dreadful mistake.

Then, there are some men that marry purely for the convenience of having someone who wears a maid's apron and a chef's hat. Someone, who cooks, cleans house and is willing to pick up the other's dirty laundry. A tax "write off" or something, or maybe they are looking forward to the little "write offs" that eventually show up along the way.

There are also women like me, who want to be loved, be married, and raise a family. I wanted someone I could share the rest of my life with. Someone, who would take care of me, as I would him, growing old together and becoming that one heart that two are supposed to be. But I was too quick to fall for someone without getting to know him as well as I should have.

Who knows what goes through some heads? Makes you wonder what they were thinking in the first place. Gee, why can't couples realize they need to work on everything together? It should not be a "yours" or "mine" proposition, but rather an "ours." It is you and me, baby, and if we hold on to each other and keep our eyes on the Lord, we can weather any storm, or at least we can give it a good try.

I do believe God allows many marriages to take place so He can work in one or both partners. He has performed great miracles in broken people and marriages that have become utter disasters. But what happens when the abused has taken all that they can possibly take and just can't do it anymore. No matter how they have tried or how long or how hard they have strived at making it work, the love and respect is just plain gone. It is really difficult to stay with someone when the physical and emotional love has become so crushed and smothered that all respect has dissolved and dissipated. It's almost like trying to breathe while in a dirt filled, vacuum bag. It just does not work!

There is obviously a real problem in too many marriages today and I have come to realize and truly believe the reason is that Jesus is probably not in those marriages. Jesus should be first on the husband's priority list, as well as on the wife's priority list. Nothing will work or even come close to a satisfying union if He has not been given the front row seat within that marriage. Even if two people that claim they don't know God or refuse to even want a personal relationship with the Lord Jesus Christ, still have many principles written on their hearts and in their conscience by God. *"But this is the new agreement I will make with the people of Israel, says the Lord: I will write my laws in their minds so that they will know what I want them to do without my even telling them, and these laws will be in their hearts so that they will want to obey them, and I will be their God and they shall be my people"* (Hebrews 8:10.)

I truly believe the heart of a man reflects what's in his soul and it is displayed through his mouth and actions, or might I say... "Apples don't grow on banana trees!" This principle spoke loudly and became meaningful to me in my marriage, when my heart began questioning the way I was being treated through the years.

I Peter 3:7 says, *"You husbands must be careful of your wives, being thoughtful of their needs and honoring them as the weaker sex. Remember that you and your wife are partners in receiving God's blessings, and if you don't treat her as you should, your prayers will not get ready answers."* Of course, treating your spouse as you should applies to wives as well, and the importance of treating one another as God intends for us to, cannot be overstated.

Love, encouragement, respect, compassion, and empathy, mixed with a continual willingness to forgive in patient tolerance, I believe is how the Lord expects us to treat others, especially our spouses. Unfortunately, it just won't catch the train to "Blessingsville" in our marriages, if we aren't submitting to Jesus and making sure He is at the forefront of our lives doing the conducting.

I once had a sticker that read *What Would Jesus Do?* I know that sticker, WWJD, can be found on just about everything and almost everywhere one looks, but I feel it has become so used; so common place as just another sticker, that it has lost its deeper meaning. If we truly asked ourselves this question, What Would Jesus Do? whenever difficult situations or people come our way. I think it would really cause us to think twice how we speak to someone or how we might treat others, and that is completely true for the married couple. You just cannot take your spouse for granted and get away without some conflict coming between.

In Ecclesiastes 4:12, it reads, *"for a triple-braided cord is not easily broken."* (There's that triple braided cord again!) Husbands, love your wives as Jesus loved the Church and wives, love, honor and respect your husband as you would the Lord. I am not talking perfection, here, but rather willingness on the part of both husband and wife, to put Christ first and a willingness to yield to one another, with all respect. Jesus is the third cord that is braided along with the husband and wife. It's a joint commission here, folks, or better put, it's a surrender to Christ first and then to each other.

Sadly, there are spouses that don't understand or care to understand that they need the Lord, but rather choose to lord it over their spouse and eventually the children, which opens the door to an intrusion of behaviors that can eventually lead to the destruction of the family and marriage.

Control, anger, rage, and abuse, whether physical, verbal, emotional or sexual, all of these behaviors can quickly consume and destroy a relationship or a family like wildfire. And if it continues without any conviction or a decision to change, no matter how often you forgive your spouse or look the other way, the marriage will disintegrate faster that ashes being washed down a drain. And what is so incredible is that too many marriages today are in this situation, and we keep asking the same question, "Why"?

What is happening to the Family Unit today? Besides the breakdown and destruction of our morals, that are obviously decaying in our world today, I believe many of these behaviors stem from unresolved issues that had developed during the growing up years of one or both spouses. Issues, no one cared enough to correct or address in those early years.

I have talked with many young couples that admit to having anger and control issues, and many of them have confessed to having had a torrent relationship with their dad and/or mom. Whether for economic hardships, lifestyles, or maturity difficulties, somehow it all impacted the nurturing of children within a family.

Many couples have shared with me that one parent or both parents were alcoholics or addicted to drugs, leading them to an inability to constructively lead their family. Many grew up with elder grandparents because their dad and/or mom where in prison and there was no one else interested enough to take care of the children, or one parent ran off, abandoning the family and the other went into a direction of careless and destructive "give up".

Sadly, many grandparents, who have been left with this responsibility, are no longer physically or psychologically capable of raising children all over again. Their love for the children may not be in question, but the emotional duress takes a huge toll.

The ability to handle a situation or effectively discipline and counsel their grandchildren is a more difficult task that can and will lead the grandparent to such frustration that they often succumb to just looking the other way.

Several have shared that their dad or mom had a terrible temper and nothing they ever did was done right in their parent's sight; nothing ever satisfied the parent, no matter how hard they tried. This usually ended up with their being subjected to the parent's physical and verbal abuse. They could never measure up to the parent's expectations, which can result in great unhappiness, guilt, insecurity, not to mention the possibility of incorrigible behavior and constant rebellion because of the inattention and lack of care or unconditional love from the parent.

There are some parents who become just plain mean and angry because of how they were raised and figure if it was good enough for them to be treated cruelly, it is good enough for their kids as well. They didn't have it easy so why should their children expect anything better or different out of life.

Then, the countless number of families that have decided to divorce, causing the children to take on the ugly pain and anger of the split, and a lot of times taking on the blame as the sole reason for the divorce as well.

Many times, you'll find one parent can't handle the children but won't allow the other parent to deal with them either, which leaves the children emotionally stuck in a hole of confusion. Often, for whatever reason, children are passed on to other relatives; shuffled back and forth from one uncle to an aunt or to a grandparent and so on. It goes on and on and on.

You may be asking, wait a minute, aren't we talking about marriage? Yep, you've got it, and a lot of the time, this is where it all begins. These unresolved issues that are brought into the marriage create dissention and destruction and as we know, children do learn what they have been taught. As in Proverbs 22:6, *"Train up a child in the way he should go, and when he is old he will not depart from it."* And again, in Ephesians 6:4, we read, *"And now a word to you parents. Don't keep on scolding and nagging your children, making them angry and resentful. Rather, bring them up with the loving discipline the Lord himself approves, with suggestions and godly advice."*

This is all sound advice from God's Word, but many do not realize that their actions and the way they speak to one another is what children learn. We really do not have to sit our children down and instruct them to listen to lessons on how to abuse and destroy others. Nope, they watch and learn, and this observed and learned behavior will become the child's lesson for life unless someone steps in and addresses this behavior and teaches the child differently.

"How does a man become wise? The first step is to trust and reverence the Lord! Only fools refuse to be taught. Listen to your father and mother. What you learn from them will stand you in good stead; it will gain you many honors" (Proverbs 1:7-9.) Children who are indifferent to authority, disrespectful and hateful, and think that swearing is the New English and the norm in communication, usually learn a lot of their behavior from their parents and peers and if it is from the parents, where is the correction, where is the wholesome example?

It has been said children are the mirror image of their parents. If this is true, just who is going to teach children the truths in life and dare to be the mirror image for the child's best welfare if it isn't the parents or some parent figure that genuinely cares and is willing to step up to the plate?

We teach our children our ways and they grow up and act just like they were taught. If that teaching has been with the disciplined love and correction of the Bible, then there will be many rewards for the child and the parent. But for some parents, who have failed to bring their children up with that disciplined love and correction; the committed desire to train up a child in the way they should go, will wonder where their children learned such deplorable behavior? Then, to make things even worse, when those children one day marry, the cycle continues. It's a vicious cycle, like an unquenchable wildfire.

How sad indeed. Our Lord must be crying great tears watching how we live and how we teach our babies… His gifts to us.

"In my distress I called upon the Lord, and cried out to my God;
He heard my voice from His temple, and my cry entered His ears."
2 Samuel 22:7

Chapter 7

You Are Somebody, Not Nobody

As I said in the beginning, I was married for more than four decades. I have been blessed with beautiful, talented, not perfect but successful children, and am now blessed with many grandchildren and great grandchildren. I took my wedding vows very seriously and felt my marriage was definitely a "death do us part" commitment. It was not an easy life, nor are most marriages, but I can assure you that the learned fear I have been speaking of was totally real and it all resulted from my husband's unhealthy desires and choices, and an unrelenting need to control.

I truly believe control was used to safeguard his obvious fear of abandonment, of which I have previously mentioned; his need to keep from becoming abandoned from those he thought he had held close. Like so many children who feel they were abandoned by divorce, he was left with family members, to be raised and then shuffled from one uncle to another grandparent, to another aunt and so on. I guess he felt he could protect himself from any more abandonment by taking control of me and the children and anything else that meant something to him. Then, if that control was questioned or baulked at or argued with, his temper would become so aggressive that soon there would be verbal expletives flying through the air, and a physical lashing out at whatever was available or within reach to destroy.

My husband was always known as a jokester—Mr. Personality or "life of the party" sort of person—when he was around others outside of the family, but underneath there was, and still is, a very angry man and I know it is largely fueled by his memories of all he believed he went through when he was growing up. Was it a great injustice, huge neglect or has it become an excuse? I really can't say.

Through the years, whenever he would reflect back to his youth and talk about different situations that took place, it was always implied that somehow, he felt as though nobody really cared for him or he felt rejected and unloved by certain family members. The injustice and unfairness brought upon him, in his opinion, was emotionally hurtful and he seems to have held onto that picture of reality all his life.

In contrast, as far as I have been told and observed, I believe the family members that took part in his rearing did the best they could. With work and families of their own and the pressures of making a living to benefit them all, they all did the best they could; not perfect, but the best they could. I tried to point that fact out to him, whenever the subject came up, of which it did every once in a while, but he still holds such bitterness, animosity, and an inability or refusal to see it from their perspective or to even forgive what he feels was injustice.

Somehow, his emotions seemed to be locked in memories of uncaring parents and the failure of proper nurturing. I often wonder, is it enough to completely blame our parents for the way we have turned out? Is it okay to think we are messed up because we didn't get what we feel was deserved in our early years of growing up? Is it okay to think our lack—our deficiency in Godly nurturing and upbringing is completely acceptable, solely because it was not our fault? I don't think so, not for a moment.

Granted, like I have said, children reflect their parents...the mentors in the early beginnings of their lives. They learn what they have been taught. But I also believe, no matter what life has handed you, you can still make something good out of it. I believe this with all my heart, and I have tried to impress this belief on my children and grandchildren. You can turn things around and accomplish whatever you want... if you want to bad enough. You need to realize, you are somebody, not nobody!

Be positive and make a difference and know that Jesus is there for you all the time! It seems we knock our socks off trying to find the right path and have it all; our dreams, instant accomplishments and spontaneously met goals, all on a silver platter. Unfortunately, none of it will work or be blessed if it is only by our own strength. It will only work if you understand who Jesus is and seek His Will and direction in your life first. After all, He already has a plan for your life.

I, too, have struggled to chart my own path and have failed miserably. There is a scripture I often turn to because it has a way of getting my attention, time and again, Matthew 11:28-30, *"Come to Me, all you who labor and are heavy laden, and I will give you rest. Take My yoke upon you and learn from Me, for I am gentle and lowly in heart, and you will find rest for your souls. For My yoke is easy and My burden is light."* This is a truth to savor!

Unfortunately for many of us, it takes time to discover that truth, because we always know what is best for us, don't we? And we want it now and we want it our way! But He waits patiently for us to give up our stronghold and reach for His always extended hand. I can remember a moment, many years ago, while in a complete state of frustration, when nothing was going well, and I wasn't seeing any answers to my prayers about, whatever it was.

Being so distraught, I threw my bible up in the air, trying to reach the 16ft. high beam in the house. Then, when it fell back down to the floor (never reaching the beam), every marker, every piece of paper that had a scripture or song phrase on it, prayer request scribbled on a sticky note, everything… fell out, leaving my bible pages scrunched up and the binding of my bible torn. Well, I thought I could strut my tail feathers and feel accomplished in showing God my displeasure, but found them plucked instead, in total guilt, remorse and shame.

You see, God always wins! As I stood there, staring at my bible in the disgust of defeat, I heard a voice in my heart ask, "Are you finished?" And when I sniffled, "Yes", I felt a real peace wash over me that was so calming. That's when I knew I had to continue trusting Him and wait for His answers to my prayers.

When I reflect on my husband's temper, I am constantly amazed and unbelievably saddened by the amount of anger that can be held onto for so long. Such wasted time and energy that produces nothing but an unfruitful life! And too, it is extremely tragic to know there are so many holding onto this type of unfulfilling life. As mentioned before, anger that would often turn into rage is usually driven by control. If something isn't being broken, something else will be thrown across the room just to get a point across.

For many the verbal abuse—swearing, criticizing, defaming, yelling and name calling, that is always meant to break a will— seems to be their normal accepted form of communication while handling any situation.

But there is another facet of control fueled by insecurity, which can become so suspecting and suspicious that it is difficult to enjoy being around others. I learned very quickly in my marriage, that if someone else, no matter who it was, or if something else took away the attention that was supposed to be solely for him, doors would slam, and anger would lead to a loss of control and result in incredible rage.

For me, I felt nothing ever seemed to make him happy. He only saw negativity in everything, whether on the TV, how someone looked; how someone looked at him or didn't make eye contact with him. No matter whom it was or what it pertained to, there could be an expected explosion of some sort so that he could make of point of getting undivided attention. And the truth of it all is that everyone, whether friend, acquaintance or family expected that explosion every time there was some kind of occasion or family get together. Interesting, how a person can demand such attention and end up losing the attention he is striving for. It makes everyone want to go home, and they usually did with urgent necessity!

How we make our Lord sad when we do what we do because it destroys our witness to others, when we live an ungodly lifestyle. I don't care how hard you try; you cannot escape from God's all seeing and all-knowing eye. How can we praise Jesus for our salvation and all He does for us and try to witness to others by telling them how much they need Jesus Christ as Lord and Savior in their lives, and then go deliberately live an openly, sinful life with no regard to what we are projecting to others?

The book of James 3:8-10 spells it out so well. *"But no man can tame the tongue. It is an unruly evil, full of deadly poison. With it we bless our God and Father, and with it we curse men, who have been made in the similitude of God. Out of the same mouth proceed blessing and cursing. My brethren, these things ought not to be so."*

I can tell you one thing for sure. It was extremely difficult to stay positive while surrounded by constant negativity. My husband once admitted that he probably didn't know how to talk to people, so he passed the buck to me. Well, I believe it is safe to say you can guess how far that went. Not far at all, because I never handled a situation like he would have, nor did I get my point across as well as he would have.

After so many years, I began to feel broken and used up and I cannot tell you how many nights I cried to the Lord to release me—release me from this agony. I have always praised God for my blessings of children, and later grandchildren, who saw me through all of these difficult years. They were the only ones that brought sunlight into my heart and brightened my day and made my life of misery tolerable. Their love and the precious love of Jesus is what kept me going all my married years and I knew He heard my cries and saw how I struggled to bear it all. I must say, it caused me to believe that one day the Lord would step in and take over… and now He has.

It's just amazing how bitter trials and long suffering can draw you closer to the Lord, if you allow Him to take over and work everything out according to His Will for you. For me, I now realize Jesus is my true husband. He is protecting and guiding me and filling me with such love and I am experiencing the joy and peace that surpasses all understanding that only Jesus can give.

Like I have said, I may not be able to see ahead, especially when my path seems incredibly rocky and totally uncertain, but the one thing I do know for sure is that my Lord is holding my hand and walking with me, not against me. And, more importantly, He will never abuse me or hurt me. I can count on that, and I want you to know He is your guarantee of peace, fulfillment, and joy as well.

"And my God shall supply all your need
according to His riches in glory by Christ Jesus"
Philippians 4:19

Chapter 8

Adjusting My Sails

After 20 years into my marriage, God opened the doors for me to go forward with a decision to attain my nursing degree. Only my Lord can do that; really! It has been mentioned more than once, the surprise of my being allowed to pursue such a huge venture, under the circumstances of living in such a difficult marriage. So, when I give all the credit to my Lord, you can understand my gratitude.

After graduating from nursing school and passing my Boards, the Lord opened the doors for a position in a hospital working on the Maternity and Surgical units. I was there for 17 years as a nurse and loved my work immensely. I was 53 years old when I started working as a nurse and never dreamed that I would be able to work long enough to receive some sort of retirement. Of course, it is a very modest retirement, given the late start of a career and the few years that I worked. But more than that, it was the blessed opportunity to serve others in this capacity and for that, I am extremely grateful to the Lord.

This work, just like my children, kept me going and it gave me purpose and a positive fulfillment like nothing else could. And not only a personal fulfillment, but it had become my escape, an opportunity to work all the hours I could get. Whether someone wanted a day off or they became too ill to come to work. Just the thought of going to work brightened my day and brought such joy to my heart. It helped me gain confidence in myself and to know I had the ability and knowledge of a professional. I was shown respect because I respectfully served others first, and then eventually I realized I could begin to respect myself.

One of the many cherished nuggets I hold in my heart came from a very special mentor. One day, while expressing the joy and love I had for my work and the great sadness I was feeling over announcing my retirement, she said, "You really don't know how much you have touched people's lives around here, do you?"

Upon hearing her make that statement, I remembered that every one of my workdays was given to God, including the many patients I would care for. I always asked the Lord to bless each and every one of them, and to fill me with His sweet Holy Spirit that I might represent His love to everyone I worked with or came into contact with, but particularly to the sick and dying.

I guess I had never looked at my work from her vantage point, so it really humbled and blessed my heart in a very surprising way, and I hold on to that moment dearly.

My work gave me such a special joy knowing I could bring a smile to someone's face or hug someone that was hurting, without my being suspected of flirting or looking for someone else other than my spouse.

I find it so interesting how my home life conditioning would even be considered in relation to my work. I could listen and give an answer, without feeling like I was stupid or ignorant, not knowing what I was talking about or worry that I had somehow said something wrong. I had a chance to breathe; breathe confidence. I had the freedom to give of myself without being criticized.

Yes, my career was a shot in the arm, no pun intended, a breath of fresh air. But when my day at work ended and as I drove out of the hospital parking lot to go home, I became increasingly aware that I was now on my way home to my unbearable torment.

Unfortunately, my wonderful world of nursing did end with retirement; retirement that I truly felt was needed at the time. I did not want to retire when I did, but I felt the Lord was leading me to make this decision. Of course, now I realize if I hadn't retired when I did, I would not have been able to leave my marriage without the ties to a job that might hold me back. Gee, that sounds like a pathetic and self-pitying excuse! Not really, because I didn't feel like I pitied myself at all, nor was I angry or blaming anyone else for having to make that decision.

I truly loved my work and would have continued working for as long as I could, but something kept gnawing at me and telling me it was time to retire, it was time to go and although I was somewhat disappointed with that thought, I was yielding myself to the Lord and what He wanted for me. Goodness, I have realized that "walking on water" is truly a lesson in faith. I am always telling others, "Just put your blinders on and trust Jesus", and now I have to listen to my own advice!

I didn't fully understand why the Lord would have me make that move and I remember feeling a little apprehensive, but I had that peace that surpasses all understanding. I found myself asking, "What if it wasn't the Lord calling me to do this, but myself?" Sometimes, or should I say often times, in questioning a leading but not knowing where it's coming from or why, we may wonder "Is that from the Lord or is it me... or is it the enemy."

I knew I had peace, because He is the only one that can give peace, and the Lord, through the Holy Spirit, had even given me a scripture to confirm it, as only He can do, Psalm 81:6, *"Now I will relieve your shoulder of its burden; I will free your hands from their heavy tasks."* It is interesting, when that scripture jumped off the page, I immediately thought, "But wait a minute, my work is not a burden or a heavy task."

It wouldn't be until it was pointed out to me, that the scripture was not speaking of my work, but of my life of unhappiness. That explanation caused a whole new eye opener! All I could do was trust Him and strive to leave my emotions out of it. Philippians 4:6 says, *"Be anxious for nothing, but in everything by prayer and supplication, with thanksgiving, let your requests be made known to God; and the peace of God, which surpasses all understanding, will guard your hearts and minds through Christ Jesus."* And that is what I did.

Believe me, that alone was such a difficult lesson to learn, but now I know it was the Lord impressing upon me the need to give up my beloved work, and that is what I did. I have come to realize in my life journey with my Savior, that He doesn't always point out the "what's and whys" ahead of time. It truly is stepping out onto the water by faith, trusting He has you and He knows exactly what He is doing.

Unfortunately, after nine months of being home, the explosive episodes grew more frequent, and it became more of puzzlement for me as to why. Retirement is supposed to be an enjoyable accomplishment shared by husband and wife; an awaited chapter of life, meant to slow everything down so we could take the time to relax and smell the flowers, and spend more quality time with each other.

I repeat; that is what retirement is supposed to be. Of course, that was not to be within the realm of our marriage, and I think that is one of many things that have broken my heart. I tried to be more attentive and helpful to him, but it seemed fireworks were always going off for some reason and I felt I was beginning to build on an unfeeling false motion of obedience to my husband.

Uncontrolled emotions began to build in my heart; feelings of hate, rejection and disrespect, and that blanket of oppression and unhappiness, that my work had seemed to lighten throughout my career, was becoming heavier until the moment of decision presented an opportunity and I jumped at it and moved on. Or should I say I moved out! Of course, it was not without a heated confrontation, of which I shudder in remembering, now. I have learned that I am a "Golden Retriever" type of personality... avoid all uncomfortable confrontation at all costs, right? Not this time! I was done. I had had enough of his abuse and constant volatility and with one rage too many from him, the Lion in me reared and that would be my final day.

As previously mentioned, I once heard a pastor on the Christian radio station talk about abuse and the many ways a lot of men, and women too, treat their spouses. He was talking specifically to men, but I feel it was meant for everyone within hearing. He said, "Men, you need to stop abusing your wives because if you keep at it, one day they are going to snap and you will never get them back!" I guess that was exactly where I had gotten to – the end of my rope and I finally snapped.

It is so sad that it had to come to this, but there must be a time when all the continual torment stops. When I think back, there were many times I had tried to convey to my husband, my concerns over the stress that was mounting in our marriage. I felt it, and I would be completely dumbfounded if he didn't as well. But I eventually realized he either didn't seem to have a clue or, he did have a big clue but chose to strengthen his grip on me in order to change it or redirect it.

I even took a great leap with a deep breath, on one occasion, and told him I felt he was two people in one body. One of them I could live with because he was nicer and calmer, but definitely not the other, of which was the controlling angry side which seemed to always take the lead over the more pleasant side. I even suggested maybe we could see a doctor to find out if there was something out of balance (I really had to choose my words wisely with that suggestion), where medication might help calm him or something, anything. Of course, that suggestion was resisted and went nowhere fast. At any rate, our talks seemed to be of no avail, and I felt we were right back where we left off.

I remember continually praying—for two solid years, that God would release me from all of this; this cruel rage filled hateful bondage I had been held in for all my married life. But I discovered, praying that God would intervene and release me was not enough. He wanted something from me as well. I knew deep in my heart's conscience, I had to tell God that I forgave my husband for all he had ever done to me, our marriage, and our family.

You see, I realized that if I did not forgive my husband, God would not forgive me for all I needed forgiveness for in my life. I also knew that if I held onto all that garbage and allowed bitterness to take root, of which was obviously developing, it would not only destroy me, but I could never get to a place where

God could bless me or even work in me. Hebrews 12:15, *"Watch out that no bitterness takes root among you, for as it springs up it causes deep trouble, hurting many in their spiritual lives."*

The Holy Spirit will not and cannot occupy the same space with evil, with sin. God was not edified in our marriage because of sin and because there was never any change or any sign of wanting to change, there was no blessing; there was no healing of our marriage bond. I had to release him into God's hands, and I admit that was a resistant choice within itself.

I remember the day, while banging my knees (that's what I call kneeling) before the Lord, He asked me, "Would you forgive him? Not because you want to; not because you feel like it, and not because you feel he deserves it, but would you forgive him because I asked you to?" I listened intently, being in awe that my Lord Jesus was asking me a direct question; a question that really put me at alert because it was soul searching. Allowing that question to sink into my hearts ears, I said, "Yes, Lord. I will forgive him, but not because I want to; certainly not because I feel like it, and definitely not because I feel he deserves it! I will forgive him because You asked me to."

I can remember asking God many times to forgive him, but when I prayed that prayer that particular day (I cannot even tell you the date or time), I mentally saw a replay of everything he ever did to me; every vile word he had ever spoken to me, and I was able to forgive him of each and every one. Have you ever experienced seeing your whole life pass before your eyes? Well, that is what I experienced with all the words and actions that had lacerated my heart all those married years.

Then, the most amazing feeling came over me; a realization I had never experienced before. I quickly felt a release off my shoulders that I cannot quite describe. It was a huge lifting of a very heavy weight, almost like an imagined backpack filled with bricks, tons of them. I mean, it just flew off my shoulders! I just don't know how else to describe it, but I really felt I had released my husband into my Father's hands, and that gave me such a tremendous relief and immense joy.

God had him now and one day, he would finally know God, at least that was my continual prayer. I knew God had His hand on me as well. I felt like I was free. Even now, as I write these words, my eyes fill with tears; tears of relief, tears of freedom, but mostly tears of great sadness. I was being hid in God's precious and protecting wings, Psalm 91:4 *"He will shield you with his wings! They will shelter you. His faithful promises are your armor."* That is just an awesome reality! He was in God's hands now and I knew!

Speaking of forgiveness and our need to do so, I have just realized a new perspective of this need. I truly believe God wants us to forgive those who have hurt us just like He teaches, but it just opened my eyes to the fact that forgiving someone who has hurt me is not just for them. It is for me, too!

My forgiving him opened the doors for God to do surgery on my heart so I could move forward. Gee, no wonder I felt the heaviness of that backpack, when it flew off my shoulders so fast! I know that's why God's word is living, and it is new every day. The Bible is His Living Word.

"Be still and know that I am God."
Psalm 46:10

Chapter 9

Standing Three Feet Taller

Well, I hurdled over a very monumental mountain; a mountain of control that locked me in a marriage that would not allow me to stand up for myself; to be the one of two voices that were supposed to have become one, on the day we married. But now, I have learned that I do have a voice and I am gaining the courage to say, "No, you can't treat me like this anymore."

My destructive marriage needed a breath of fresh air; a fresh coat of paint, if you will, and it was painting me out of the picture! Now I finally have the courage to stand up for myself and with

God's hand holding onto mine, I am beginning to walk toward self-respect and confidence. I am finally realizing I do have worth and do not have to be controlled anymore, and I can't tell you how good that feels.

Of course, all the hard work is ahead of me, but I have the Lord to help me with that. Jesus has shown me that He has a plan for me. Jeremiah 29:11, *"For I know the plans I have for you, says the Lord. They are plans for good and not for evil, to give you a future and a hope."* He has a plan for my life and for right now, all I am expected to do is rest and trust in Him.

I am not saying it is easy, going through the emotional stress of knowing where I have come from and not have a clue of what I am doing, much less where I am going. Then, to just sit and rest and try not to focus on the hurdles that lay ahead, can be quite frustrating, especially when my determination wants to try and figure it all out.

To just wait upon the Lord takes a true lesson in patience and to allude to this being an easy task couldn't be further from the truth. The Lord has told me to rest in Him, trusting that He has already gone before me and prepared my way; my victory has been sealed and when it is time to make a move, He would show me and lead me in that direction.

It has really been quite difficult at times, more often than not, but it's a matter of holding on to Jesus and following His instructions. He knows what's ahead of me, whereas I don't, and just knowing that He really does love me and promised never to leave me, makes it easier to breathe in that assurance that I will be okay.

As I have always said, "Just put your blinders on", but now I am realizing just what that means. It's having faith that the Lord has everything under control, His control, and He will give me victory if I look to Him for it. Not only will He give me the victory that I need, but I have also come to know that He is my victory; therefore, I do not have to focus upon some kind of tangible or visual victory itself, as we all seem to reach for. Does that make sense?

We look to Him as our victory first and then that He will unveil that particular, tangible or visual victory. I had to let that truth sink in for a while, because it took me time to really understand the depth of what that really meant. I found, that when I opened my heart to Jesus and let it all lay bare—my marriage, my trial, my heartache, what I wanted and what I didn't want—I knew He had me, my trial and my life and He had already secured that victory. Isaiah 43:1-3, *"But now the Lord who created you, O Israel, says, Don't be afraid, for I have ransomed you; I have called you by name; you are mine. When you go through deep waters and great trouble, I will be with you. When you go through rivers of difficulty, you will not drown! When you walk through the fire of oppression, you will not be burned up-the flames will not consume you. For I am the Lord your God, your Savior, the Holy One of Israel."*

You see, He has gathered and held onto all the broken pieces of my life and is creating something victoriously new out of all those pieces. He secured mine and I hope you know He has gone before each and every one of His children, when they go through the deep waters of oppression and affliction and secured all victories. I want you to know He has all your broken pieces in His hands, and He will never let you down.

There is a song we sing in church, which speaks of our need to walk by faith, even when we can't see what's ahead. God knows how broken our lives are and He uses those broken pieces to prepare His Will for us. Yes, it has been a real struggle to let go and just wait on the Lord, but I do know He is aware of what we all have gone through, and He is very aware of what He wants to take place in our lives.

I am reminded of Matthew 10:29-31, *"Not one sparrow (what do they cost, two for a penny?) can fall to the ground without your Father knowing it. And the very hairs of your head are all numbered. So don't worry! You are more valuable to Him than many sparrows."*

I know this to be true, but it is amazing how I can go from being so confident and trusting, to becoming a mound of unstable Jell-O! Just amazing how our faith struggles to stand firm! It is so comforting, though, knowing that He knows us so well. But then, why shouldn't He? He created us, didn't He? And, because He was tempted as we are, He definitely knows our weaknesses. And He even knows when we are going to change from trusting to turning into that mound of unstable Jell-O!

I have always felt I had the greatest of patience for just about anyone and anything, but I have found that is not some sort of guarantee because I have wrestled greatly with patience since this huge chapter of my life began. Then the doubt that drifts in like a heavy fog and seems to swallow everything up, until I feel like I can't see clearly or even breathe, for that matter.

I have been over wrought with sadness, with a faucet that is hidden somewhere in my head that doesn't seem to be equipped with a shut off valve to stop the flowing tears, and a deep dark hole of depression that has not provided a ladder for climbing out! Too many nights find too little if no restful sleep. Does this sound familiar? The searching for answers and the constant crying out to God, "What is happening? What am I supposed to do?"

Sometimes I feel like we all tend to look for a great big billboard in the sky, spelling it all out explicitly, but there is none. Or maybe anticipate a big blasting voice from heavens megaphone, telling us where to go and when to go... But go where? And then, after we have exhausted ourselves from fretting, of which we are told not to in Psalm 37:7, *"Rest in the Lord, and wait patiently for Him; Do not fret because of him who prospers in his way, because of the man who brings wicked schemes to pass,"* screaming loud enough for the whole block to hear, then continually pound our head into a tear-soaked pillow, He will answer, and His peace seems to pour over your head and down to your toes, melting the anguish with calm. That is exactly what happens to me.

Whether through a scripture or something I read in my devotional, my spirit will be uplifted with words of encouragement; encouragement to go on. You know how that is, when God uses just about anything; a little something to speak to you. It is just incredible how much our Lord loves us and sees what we are going through.

I once heard a pastor on a Christian program say, "Those who are to be blessed must constantly be broken." That is how God works things out in our lives. He uses the troubles, the trials; the sadness, tragedies and catastrophes in our lives, not only to help us get through those times, but to pave a way for us to be able to help someone else that may be going through the same type of trial, and this is the very reason I am writing my book!

2 Corinthians 1:3-4 says, *"Blessed be the God and Father of our Lord Jesus Christ, the Father of mercies and God of all comfort, who comforts us in all our tribulation that we may be able to comfort those who are in trouble, with the comfort with which we ourselves are comforted by God."* It has forever been quoted that God helps those who help themselves, but that is not how God works. He helps those who cry out to Him and by faith trust Him to help.

God, in His great love, has not only brought me out of my bondage, but is guiding, protecting, and providing for me as well as teaching me along a path that I believe has been set before me in order to reach His intended purpose. Jeremiah 29:11 was not meant just for me. It was meant for all who are searching for purpose or wondering what this life has for them! It is a truer than true message for all who will believe it and cling to it.

Have you felt as though you have been all used up and there was nothing left, like I do? I know there are so many women who feel the same, going through the aftermath of all the hideous guilt and brokenness brought upon them. It seems difficult to even imagine that there may be sunlight at the end of this dark tunnel that has consumed all our dreams. All those years are gone and sometimes I can't help but feel those years were all for not.

Like in Isaiah 49:4, *"Then I said, 'I have labored in vain, I have spent my strength for nothing and in vain"* And then I read Jeremiah 31:16, *"Refrain your voice from weeping, and your eyes from tears; for your work shall be rewarded, says the Lord, and they shall come back from the land of the enemy."* I guess it is a human response, feeling all used up by disappointment and heartache, but He has shown me it was and will be all worth it because it was not a huge mistake.

My love for Jesus and the sharing of my faith to my children and to my husband during all those years, even if I feel they may not have listened, will one day be rewarded. You see my deepest and most heartfelt and continual prayer is for each of them to see their need for Jesus, to call upon Him and have a desire to live for Him; to fall in love with our Redeemer and discover they can have a personal relationship with Him.

There is a blessing waiting for me and I can't tell you how much I look forward to that. I may not know in what capacity that blessing will be, but it will be worth it because it will be from my Lord Jesus. All I have to do is keep my eyes on Him and trust Him to take care of me. You know, it is "putting those blinders on" while He makes all things new. Isaiah 43:18, 19, *"Do not remember the former things, nor consider the things of old. Behold, I will do a new thing, now it shall spring forth; shall you not know it? I will even make a road in the wilderness and rivers in the desert."*

I cannot say I have journeyed upon an easy path, because it has been anything but, and I also know that many women have labored longer and harder through a life more devastating than mine. What I can attest to, is that the Lord has taught me so many things along the way; so many lessons have had to be learned and those lessons have often been extremely difficult and painful. Yes, painful, and more than I care to experience, but I truly believe the Lord is leading me forward because He isn't finished with me yet. I haven't arrived yet, so to speak.

I also believe He wants to make my feet like hinds' feet so that I am able to climb the crevices, in order to reach and take hold of all that He has for me as it says in Habakkuk 3:19, *"The Lord God is my strength, and He will make my feet like Hinds' Feet, and He will make me to walk upon mine High Places."*

In 2015, while reading my daily devotional, the emotional breakdown that seemed to be looming within my heart for a while came to a head (for the umpteenth time), and the flood gates opened with the deep cry of frustration. I cried out "Lord, how can I possibly follow you up this mountain, while this burden I can't seem to let go of, is becoming terribly heavy and hindering my steps, and I just can't seem to keep up." At that moment, His incredibly sweet and compassionate voice said, "Give it to me and I will carry it for you." Mind you, He did not say, "Just leave it" or "Just put it down and forget it". No. He knows my burdens are heavy and as much as He would like for me to leave them behind, He loves me enough to let me know He understands and will carry my load for me.

As you can imagine, my heart just melted again, and I deposited more tears in that bottle of mine! I know many have experienced His love in moments like this. Jesus is not a taskmaster. He said His yolk is easy, and His love and deep compassion and understanding are always available, for all who would call upon His name.

*"Then you will lie down in peace and safety, unafraid;
and I will bind you to me forever with chains of
righteousness and justice and love and mercy."*
Hosea 3:18-19

Chapter 10

It Doesn't Really Matter, Does It?

Okay, what now? Now that all the dust has found a semblance
of settling and my life's pieces have all been strewn about, as if
a hurricane had just flown through the remains of all the broken
cookie crumbs of dreams and then deposited them in a torrent
of places. Bewildered, as I look around, all that can be seen is the
worst mess a lifetime of playful, mischievous, fun-loving children,
added with total chaos, has ever been recorded as creating… Now
what? What do I do now? What can I do now?

I am sure we all can testify to a horrendous mess in our lives,
at one time or another, right? Well, I suppose I could say, "When

life gives you more lemons than you can use, have a cupcake...or make some! Really? Maybe, but I am happy to write that I have finally realized the answer to this life-filled waste of emotional, physical, and spiritual havoc, pain and energy.

You return to the answer that was there all along and sits on top of the nucleus of it all... you and the Lord God, your Maker! And you keep those blinders on in trust and don't take them off for an instant because Jesus is making all things new! After all, we ask Him to, don't we? Maybe not in so many words, but when we cry out to Him for help and believe He has a better way; that is like asking Him for all the new He has for us. Honestly, it is better than the old that keeps us buried in bondage.

It has been four years since I left the life I had been bound to for so long and almost three years since the Lord directed me to make a long distance move to another state. As I consider all that has happened and all the many lessons that have been presented along the way, I realize it takes time to focus on new redirected, rejuvenated life.

How often we tend to squirm and become fidgety and discover impatience (ah ha, and I thought I held the edge on patience!) screaming "get on with it" and "get me out of here." We tend to want to get through the forest of learning as quickly as possible... if only all those trees weren't holding us back and getting in the way of our immediate success! But really, the problem with that, rushing to get through that forest, is that the learning is cheated out of a purposeful lesson.

I have also become extremely aware that it takes an awful long time to heal. Moments of hurt and disbelief seem to drift past my memory bank more often than I care to endure, and it doesn't take much to set it all off to remember, rehash and pine over, resulting in self-pity. You know what I mean? It can be a scene from a movie, a certain song, a memory from Christmas or birthday past or just a remembered scent that drifted past my heart's memory. It could even be a remembered confrontation, a word, or a situation that you might wish had never happened or had taken place. I'm sure you know how that goes.

I think the most trying and regrettable thoughts are of a marriage that wasn't supposed to turn out the way it did. It's the growing old together and walking through the "nuances of life", so they say on the tv commercials, with your mate, that you feel cheated out of. Have you ever watched a couple interacting with one another and suddenly find yourself mentally playing out the outcome of a similar interaction from your past? What you are watching, in real time, turns out completely opposite of what your memory may remember, and it can just plain break your heart knowing it could have been so different, so beautifully different. But, after my thoughts torture me for a while, and I consider that even though it matters, it really doesn't matter, I remember that God is very much aware of what is in my heart and what I am feeling, and He isn't looking the other way. And, more importantly, He is allowing the time it takes for me to learn to trust Him.

The time it takes to allow Him to heal all areas of my life and to build my confidence in His leading. I have discovered that trials are not so much what happens to you, as they are what you do with them; what you learn from them. Besides being my Savior, my Lord and best friend, He is my husband now and I am learning that He has my best interest in full focus and will allow anything that is going to cause my faith to grow more dependent upon His love.

We soon realize that, slowly but surely, we are getting a little closer to the top of the mountain where our past loved ones have reached. They know how rough a terrain it is, and they were victorious with their travel upon the rugged path that had been placed before them. Paul refers to our life walk as a race. Hebrews 12:1-2 states, *"Therefore we also, since we are surrounded by so great a cloud of witnesses, let us lay aside every weight, and the sin which so easily ensnares us, and let us run with endurance the race that is set before us, looking to Jesus, the author and finisher of our faith, who for the joy that was set before Him endured the cross, despising the shame, and has sat down at the right hand of the throne of God."*

I don't know if our past loved ones are watching our progress from their vantage point or not. Frankly, I think they are enjoying and rejoicing just in knowing where they are. I know I would! But I do believe Paul is explaining that the heroes of the Bible, those who have gone on before us, have run their race and won because of their faith and witness and determination. Because they endured all they went through to reach their goal, we have the same opportunity to reach ours; the same chance to win our awaited trophy as well. After considering this truth, I have realized there is a flip side to "it doesn't matter."

You see, it does too really matter! All that we have gone through in our faith walk, through all the trials and tribulations; the failures and mistakes, the sins that cause us such grief…it matters because Jesus cares about our lives and all we have been through, and when we come before His throne and hand over our will for Him to change, He does just that. I know for sure Jesus is not only cheering us on, but He is holding our hand, especially when we slip or fall on all those rocks and boulders, and it is His intention that we make it over the finish line.

I guess the next question would be, "What have I learned so far, traveling on this path of mine? And now that I have entered a new door, what have I learned that gives me new strength and clarity and what can I share that would help someone else?" Again, 2 Corinthians 1:4, *"who comforts us in all our tribulation, that we may be able to comfort those who are in any trouble, with the comfort with which we ourselves are comforted by God."*

"Trust in the Lord with all your heart, and lean not on your own understanding; In all your ways acknowledge Him, and He shall direct your path."
Proverbs 3:5-6

Chapter 11

Independently Dependent

I find the need to remind myself, from time to time, that four decades is a very long time and new is just that... New. It is different. It hasn't been experienced yet and it will take a while to embrace and accept. And it is going to take my willingness to face it all with courage. Like I have said, marriage is for keeps. It is a covenant made before God and a promise to one another, that through thick and thin, for better or for worse (and believe me there may be far worse than better), the husband and wife keep hold of one another's hands and don't let go. I think this is the hardest truth to let go of, because the situation I had lived in led to a door of departure.

It still hurts deeply because it wasn't supposed to be this

way. But, since this is the way it is and I know my Lord Jesus has not left my side, I can say I have learned many things from this experience. First of all, and most important, I am learning more and more each day that because Jesus is my husband now, He won't hurt me, forsake me, or betray me, as what happened before with my former husband. Hosea 2:20 says, *"I will betroth you to me in faithfulness and love, and you will really know me then as you never have before."*

Okay, lesson time: I believe one of the biggest lessons is twofold. First, it is keeping my eyes on Jesus and not on my understanding. And second, not looking solely to someone else for guidance, or trusting the significance of a situation unless my Lord has directed it.

My heart holds another nugget from many years ago… 1975 to be exact. One day, I was sewing dresses for my two little girls. My husband was at work and the girls were upstairs playing tea party with their dolls. While sitting downstairs at my sewing machine, I heard the Lord's voice. I say it was Him, because of the tone that was used and the attention it commanded, the words spoken, and the pure fact that I was all alone. There was no music playing on the radio, no one in the room with me, only my eyes watching the needle of the machine stitching up and down across the fabric, focused on keeping those stitches straight. He said, "There is power in My name; use it."

Needless to say, I stopped what I was doing, looked around the room, as if expecting to see the person who had just said what

I heard! Then again, I heard, "There is power in My name; use it." That was, I believe, the very first time I heard the Lord speak to my heart audibly, since I had my "fall in love with Jesus" experience in 1972, and I have held onto those words since then. He caused my thoughts to wrap around the fact that He was with me all the time and that I could truly trust in Him, and I could use His name whenever I needed Him. I could call upon Him, trusting He was near— to ask that a fever would leave my baby's body, and it instantly did; to dislodge the grain of bran stuck in the throat of my cow (we once ran a farm) of which it did... with a big gulping swallow, or to command in His name, a spirit of fear from the enemy, to leave, and it did.

You see, He is Alive, He is always near, and we can do nothing without Him. Jesus is our strength, and His promises can be trusted. He is Truth, He is the Way, and He is the Life, and it is all ours for the asking. One of my most favorite scriptures in the Bible is Deuteronomy 30:20, *"that you may love the Lord your God, that you may obey His voice, and that you may cling to Him, for He is your life and the length of your days."*

The next lesson has to be one of the most important we will ever learn and that is forgiveness. But let's back up for just a moment and talk about trials. Just like all of you, it seems like I have gone through endless trials in my faith walk in life— trials of all kinds, all sizes and of many different degrees of breaking. I think you may know what I am talking about, and we can all agree we could write a book... Right?

As mentioned before, I once heard on a Christian radio station, "Those who are to be blessed must constantly be broken." Not sure if that brings anyone great comfort. Well, I truly believed the condition of my married life and the decision to leave it was about as big of a trial imaginable, and it tested my courage and trust in Jesus like nothing else I could have ever thought possible. It took every ounce and iota of strength to hold onto my Lord's hand with faith and trust, knowing He was holding onto my hand as well. He guided and nurtured and fed and watered and bathed me in His love throughout these 2½ years to where I am now. What a journey it has been! I truly felt I had finally taken leaps and bounds into physical, emotional, and spiritual health.

Then one day, without any warning, I felt I had been thrown back into another ugly and unbelievable trial of fire; a circumstance that knocked me down so hard, beyond my imagination, and it was about to completely destroy my integrity and the confidence, self-respect and self-worth that had just begun to build up in me after such a long drought of time.

What do you do? What can you do when you realize someone or something has blasted you with such force, stripping you of all credibility and self-esteem, slamming you spiritually right back down into a vile pit? Come on now, really?

After I had mustered up all the gritting strength I possibly could, it would be ugly cutting and questioning words, from someone close to me, someone I had always trusted that lashed out at me, filling my mind with suspicious doubt. Those suggesting words were as if their teeth were razor sharp, lacerating my heart but again. Boy, the enemy really stoops to all levels. That devil seems to love to sting us when we are just getting up from the last one, almost like a yellowjacket.

But the Lion in me has emerged from this dark pit, only to have renewed courage and an "adrenalinized" (my own word) stance in my faith, realizing Jesus has continued to hold my hand as He promised. And now, after looking this new demon in the eye, I can honestly say I feel three feet taller, and I am still growing!

Trials by fire can be exhaustingly painful when we find ourselves encapsulated within them, and all too often we exhaust ourselves searching and asking "Why, where did this come from?" It's that situation that sends shock waves through your whole body blindsiding you, leaving you feeling helpless and powerless, with no answers to justify its reasoning. It's those situations that are beyond your imagination how or why it has happened. It could be a loss of something truly important or valuable or loss of someone close to you. It could even be a wrongfully slanderous accusation and it will just leave you dumbfounded.

Then, when the numbing inability to comprehend all that just happened, the Holy Spirit embraces your heart, letting you know this is His fight not yours! That is when the love and immeasurable Grace of Lord God allows you to take a moment or a few weeks, months, or years of moments to grieve. I know this is exactly how I felt with my recent trial. The incredible helplessness mixed with the awareness that I had no strength or wisdom to handle such a situation, but He did because it was His fight. He understandably grieves with us and teaches us that He and only He is able and willing to lift us up again and change everything into good, just like Romans 8:28, *"All things work together for good to those who love God and are called according to His purposes."* (I will come back to that scripture in a while).

I have also come to realize that it is wise to pay attention to what you ask the Lord for. At a time when I had asked two things from the Lord, first "I want it all; I want all you have for me," (bring it on, right?) Second, "Can I have just a little glimpse of what you are doing?"

Well, I did not stop to consider that the reward of His Will for me; all that I had asked Him for and continue to ask Him for, would sometimes be preceded by ugly, painful, and irreprehensible fire storms of yuk that was intended to teach me and test my faith in the One who holds the universe in His hands and breathes His breath into my lungs to strengthen me.

The incredible fury, which comes up against us during a spiritual attack, can become vilely relentless, tempting us to let go of Jesus hand. While pulling us down once again into the caldron of defeat and brokenness, it is Satan's plan to destroy our trust and testimony in our Savior. But it is so comforting to know Jesus will never let go of your hand. His power is greater and His willing endurance was already displayed when He conquered the evil of our sins on the Cross. We know the end of the story and we, through our determined trust and faith in the King of Kings, our

Savior and Redeemer are branded with His name, and no one can take us away from Him.

Okay, well… I think it is safe to say we have all gone through many trials, right? And I am sure many of you have experienced the debilitating trials of fire. So now I want to get to the meat of it all, and that is forgiveness.

Within the flames of a trial, especially a trial by fire, it is God's intention that our faith be tested, refined, and purified just as gold is purified in a kiln. As the temperature increases, impurities begin to surface, allowing them to be removed and purified. That is how it is with our faith. As the dirty yuk surfaces throughout our walk with Him, it needs to be confessed and cleansed by His forgiveness and it is a continual process between us and God. But the trials of fire that lash out at us are not always because of our doing. Sometimes, they just somehow become attached to us for no other reason than to get our eyes off Jesus and cause us to stop trusting Him. It is like the devil wants to pull the rug out from under your spiritual feet to cause great harm, hurt and destruction.

Think about John 10:10, *"The thief does not come except to steal, and to kill, and to destroy. I have come that they may have life, and that they may have it more abundantly."* But know, God intends for your faith to be built up stronger so that you will have the strength to keep a tight grip on His hand and trust Him for what He wants to do for you. What Satan would take satisfaction in destroying, Jesus allows, in order to purify your faith in Him and ground you in His name. And, according to I Corinthians 10:13, *"No temptation has overtaken you except such as is common to man; but God is faithful, who will not allow you to be tempted beyond what you are able, but with the temptation will also make the way of escape, that you may be able to bear it."*

Like I said earlier, it is not pleasant going through the devastation of a fiery trial. But I feel we need to understand a trial by fire often times is held in the hands of forgiveness, presenting an opportunity to surrender to Jesus Lordship, and forgive; forgive the unforgivable. Do you know what I am talking about?

Yes, it's really difficult when we realize that this is going to have to be done, even when we want to scream out, "But, it's not fair," or "It's not my fault." I have come to realize something very interesting, if not truly comical when you think about it. We humans seem to find a need to place the wrongs and injustices others have done to us, into categories.

And we seem to categorize by titles.

(1) There are categorized cubbies for small little, if not, itty bitty sins.

(2) There are cubbies for hardly noticeable, but still counts as sins.

(3) There's a bigger cubby for the really big bad mean sins.

(4) And, even a bigger cubby for Category #1 sins (as if they were of hurricane force).

(5) Then we move into a cabinet for the unforgivable sins, because there needs to be a lot more space for these.

(6) But the Granddaddy Room (we're moving up to larger scale cubbies now) of them all is for those, twist my arm, I will forgive, BUT... I will never, ever forget sins.

Oh, my dear Lord Jesus, show us our way!

After the immediate shock and helpless devastation of my recent trial by fire, I spent a lot of time, doing that pondering thing of trying to figure out the why's and what for's of this trial; the where did this come from and the searching for answers that were so needed; an explanation for it all. I mean, really, there truly had to be an explanation for this and I was coming up empty no matter what I tried to reason! That is when my brain started to connect the dots, taking on a whole new perspective of Jesus dying on the Cross for me, for all of us.

Jesus died for forgiveness of my sins.

He died on a cross that was meant for me!

He forgave me! Period. And all I had to do was to believe it and accept it. When He said, in Mark 8:34-38, *"Whoever desires to come after Me, let him deny himself and take up his cross and follow Me,"* the important part of what He meant, was that I had to forgive; forgive the unforgivable, again, and again and again like He did me. You know that 7 times 70 thing? Ah huh, just like when I had to forgive my husband because Jesus asked me to! Psalm 51:10 says, *"Create in me a clean heart, O God, and renew a steadfast spirit within me."*

I had to get my dictionary out, because even though I knew what steadfast meant, I wanted to know how deep that meaning went. Steadfast means firm, fixed, constant (there's that 7 times 70 thing again). We read these words, but I believe we need to let these words become seeds, planted deep into our hearts and nurtured and bathed in forgiveness for those who have crushed us, that our willingness to truly forgive will be pleasing unto the Lord. Jesus went to the Cross to die a brutal and humiliating death just for us, that we might be saved, and what He said on that Cross is also what we need to do – and that is forgive!

That Cross represents Forgiveness.

Jesus asked His Father for our needed Forgiveness,

He lovingly and willingly died for that Forgiveness, and (this is the clincher, my new and deeper perspective) He said if we want to follow Him, we must carry our own cross and follow Him… in forgiving those who sin against us, whether it is our fault or not!

I still feel incredible hurt beyond all disbelief when I focus on this recent trial, taking my eyes off Jesus and trying to figure it all out again, but He continues to show me this is His fight not mine and I need to keep it right here, pointing to His eyes, "keep your eyes on Me."

I still don't understand where this trial came from or why, but like I have said before, though it matters, it really doesn't matter because the Lord is working it out for His purpose according to His plan for me and all who are involved. I also realize that even though I have unanswered questions, I'm not going to let them cause me to forget what I do know, and that is God is still on the throne.

It's like Chuck Smith used to say, "Don't give up what you do know for what you don't know." He is still in control and because He has all the answers, I don't have to be concerned with answers. Oh, and that scripture in Romans 8:28, *"All things work together for Good to those who love God and are called according to His purposes."* Well, according to His purpose, He wants to be glorified, and His Will for us is that we give Him continual praise for who He is and for the blessing He plans on giving us because of this current trial we are all going through or will go through.

Yes, He is very much aware of what we are going through; yes, He hears us when we panic and cry out to him, just like Peter did on the water; yes, He answers us and yes, He wants to work things out so He can bless us. Oh, and speaking about Peter, get your eyes off the water and on to Jesus! Remember, ultimately it is His plan, His will that He gets all the glory, because of what He wants to do for us through it. This is His battle, not mine and not yours, not ever! I knew that immediately. This was too big, and I couldn't fight it.

As 1 Samuel 17:47 states, *"the Lord does not save with sword and spear; for the battle is the Lord's."* And, because it's His fight, He is able to do exceedingly more than we could ever imagine. Like I have always preached to my children, "Let go and Let God", keep your eyes on Jesus, knowing He hears and answers and because you are branded with His name, you can trust Him. Then you too, will be able to say, "I got through this, and I am now "three feet taller" and still growing!"

"But now, O Lord, you are our Father, we are the clay,
and You our potter; and all we are the work of Your hand."
Isaiah 64:8

Chapter 12

Mirror, Mirror on the Wall

I believe it is extremely important to remember, we are all a work in progress. God is the Potter, and we are the clay, and He knows exactly how we are to be formed according to His plan. Our heart's home needs to be renovated, from time to time, so that it becomes more heavenly minded; more like our Savior, and often times it can become really uncomfortable and painful, going through the remolding and rebuilding process.

He is continually arranging, changing, and rearranging our hearts through teaching, healing, forgiving, strengthening and relationship restoring, and it can get rough and rocky quite often. But as we keep our feet grounded to the course in the race and keep our eyes focused on the final reward, realizing our biggest cheering squad, led by Jesus, is waiting for us to cross the finish line, then it will all be worth it. That thought should keep us striving to the end. I know this is what I have to keep focused on, myself.

After all those years, I stand in front of my mirror and look at the sadness in the eyes that are looking back at me. The hair is turning grayer by the minute, not to mention the wrinkles that seemed to have appeared in fast forward. I stand and wonder, as one of those tears slide down my face, knowing Jesus is about to catch it, and probably knows there will be many more within the time that I stand there starring; where did time go, and what happened to all the pretty years? It's all gone!

Then, as I look away, I find myself walking an uncharted, unfamiliar path; a path that seems downright scary, as if it might crumble under my feet if I dare take my eyes off each step. Scary, because it is just me now; all alone, so I think. It's as though I am swimming upstream but the current keeps grabbing hold of my ankles and I feel I am being dragged in a direction opposite of where I am supposed to be going, or should I say, a direction I was used to going.

Then, Jesus grabs hold of my wrist, and I am aware of my life jacket, my Savior and He allows me to see I am not alone. Yes, new is different than what we have become used to, but if the Lord is directing it and this is His path, He intends to bless our socks off with, then it is just that, a blessing! Huge!

The next equally important lesson, I have learned in my

faith walk is Agape Love. Agape is God's love for us, and it was displayed on the Cross; the Cross Jesus died on. I learned, because I had forgiven my husband, I had to Agape him, or better put, I had to allow the Holy Spirit to love him through my heart so I could pray for him through that love, on a daily basis.

You see, I can't love my husband anymore and I really don't want to, but Jesus can, and He wants to use me as a vessel to love that man through prayer, going before the throne of God on my husband's behalf. In saying that, I am reminded of the day I told my husband I had forgiven him, but he took that statement as an okay for me to come right back to him.

No, forgiving through Agape love is not returning to what God has brought you out of. I am still not sure my husband understands it all yet, but I pray he will one day. You know, Jesus still loves that man, and He isn't finished with him yet. Neither is He finished with me or with you. And when Jesus asks us to forgive and when we do, we need to see forgiveness is wrapped in the arms of Agape.

I have also learned that I could talk with my husband, because of the power of the Holy Spirit, and not have to present myself with anger. Should I be angry? Absolutely! But I couldn't hold onto that anger because I told Jesus I forgave him, and that was my word committed before the Lord.

So often I have heard women say they can't forgive the one responsible for breaking them, because they want that person to pay. They want that person to feel what it is like to be crushed the way that person crushed them. I think we all can stand on that prideful podium, huh! We want to get even, and we want them to hurt, but we are faced with a truth in God's Word, Hebrews 10:30, For we know Him who said, *"Vengeance is Mine, I will repay"*, says the Lord."

When we are able to focus on what Jesus did for us; what He cried out to His Father while He was slowly dying on that cross, Luke 23:34 *"Father, forgive them for they know not what they do,"* that is when our hearts can agree; have to agree with His words and voice the same thing.

We need to remember that our Lord went through it first and because of that, He gives us the needed strength to surrender those who have hurt us. We can't control what is needed to correct or straighten out those who have hurt us, but He can, and He will, just like He does with us when we have harmed someone. Remember, that person or persons may be totally unlovable to you and to me, but Jesus died for that person just like He did for us, and He is giving them time to choose. Besides, the greatest thing you can seek for someone who has crushed you is to pray; pray with all your heart and pray as often as you think of them. That, my friend, is one of the greatest decisions you can make, and it does please God when you do.

As I said before, in 1990, with the prompting of my daughter was when I decided to go back to school, though I was well past the age of attending school. Nonetheless, I set my heart on a new career and that was when I became a nurse on the Post-Partum Floor. And I loved every moment of it. But in 2010, after 17 years of nursing, I knew it was time to retire. It wasn't something I wanted to do, but I truly felt the Lord was directing that move. Plus, it was something my husband kept pushing for as well.

I realize now, that had been a good decision. I thank God for so much. Though there have been countless times of regret, the one thing I cannot regret are the children. Marriage is supposed to be for keeps, but I can't tell you how difficult it is when your life is filled with continual abuse. We were together for 43 years, before I finally had to leave, or I would have literally been found dead!

After enduring a four-decade long nightmare of abuse, while desperately holding onto my marriage vows no matter what, and while trying to protect my children, I had nothing left in me. I was broken, scared beyond description, and felt as if I was moving in a heavy fog. I just couldn't live like this any longer and I knew, if I stayed, I'd soon be dead. I had forced the drive to make it work for far too long, but physically I lost my strength and mentally I was numb.

My sister and brother-in-law became my buoy, and I realized my Lord was the Anchor that was holding me together. Ten years after running away, running in a new direction of safety, my Lord hasn't let go of my hand, just as He promised.

I ran away from home in 2011, and stayed with my sister and brother-in-law in Reno, Nevada, for seven months before returning to the Islands. I went back to "push buttons"… meaning, I needed to get a grasp on what I needed to do; to continue to work on my marriage or file for divorce.

I was rehired at the hospital and worked one more year, but because of fear for my life as well as the need to be with family, as my dad was dying, I packed up and finally moved back to Reno. I now have my own home and have been able to get to know my family (who live close by) after so many years being away. I was with my dad when he died three weeks after my return and since, have lost my mom and my baby brother most recently. But life goes on.

In 2013, I was hired as a counselor/advocate at the Crisis Pregnancy Center in Reno but retired from there after five years. I remain in contact with my directors and co-workers, and I am now on the Board of Directors today. I was able to get my certification in Christian Counseling and have been very active at my church, Calvary Chapel Reno Sparks.

As of today, I am leading two Women's Bibles Studies, one of which is my passion in Counseling. This door that is leading to my longtime dream of becoming a writer is now, as I speak, a reality and it has my Lord Jesus fingerprints all over it.

Having said this, I give all Praise and Glory to my Lord, as He has watched over me all my years and is taking all my broken pieces of life and making something beautiful before Him and for Him. Words cannot express how grateful I am or how blessed that I feel.

"Blessed be the God and Father of our Lord Jesus Christ, the Father of mercies and God of all comfort, who comforts us in all our tribulation that we may be able to comfort those who are in any trouble, with the comfort with which we ourselves are comforted by God."

2 Corinthians 1:3, 4

Chapter 13

Trust Changes Everything

I would like to reiterate that writing this book was not to hold my husband accountable or place blame solely on him for the failure of our marriage. Rather, this was meant to expose, from a very personal experience, what is happening in too many marriages today, and to possibly reach out to the countless women who are bound to the same pattern of living of which I have spoken. It breaks my heart knowing there are so many out there in our neighborhoods, at work and even in our churches, and to realize a large majority of these women live their horror and injustice silently, and unfortunately, that silence is screaming!

They wear that same cellophane mask I did.

Honestly, I would give anything for my marriage to have had a better outcome. I held on to that fact marriage was for better or worse and there was a lot worse, than better. But marriage is for keeps, and that is what I held onto, for as long as I possibly could. But, then again, like I have said, abuse is often silent and unspoken, but the effects are devastating as it destroys. The controller appears anything but abusive and the one abused will never let on or speak of her torment unless she has braved it and escaped from her captor.

I also know there must be many hurting women out there that may be curious about their silent world and wonder if anyone else is going through what they are experiencing. Often, a woman may feel this lifestyle is unique, solely to her. It just can't be normal or common and it leaves one wondering who in their right mind would want to live like this... if it is!

Many may be curious if there are any books to be read that might bring comfort or just plain shed some light on this way of life? It is as if you are scared to death to find out, but you desperately need to know. I say this because I was curious as well but didn't have the courage to find out. I was too afraid that I would be exposing myself if I were caught reading a book on such a matter.

I do know this brokenness you are going through has taken a huge toll, as I am proof of all I had to experience, as well. I also know that lonely feeling you may be going through right now. But I want you to take a long look in your mirror and fix your eyes on the one starring back at you and tell her to stop her crying and to believe she is somebody, not nobody. I want you to tell her she does have the strength of a warrior.

You are a strong woman of courage because remember, when you think you are weak and have no strength left to continue; you just can't do it anymore, look back at how long you have struggled through all that you have, and notice just how far you have come, and you are still standing! And because of that, dear lady, you do have the ability to take action and say, "No More!"

"Not Ever Again!"

My friend, if you are going through any of the experiences I have shared and fear being exposed or found out, my heart cries for you with great compassion, and I pray you will find the courage at the right time to leave—to run and run as fast as you can and call out for help. I know it may be your worst nightmare attempting to leave your imprisonment only to be caught by your captor, but it will be the best decision you could make if you have the help you need to keep you safe.

I want you to know there are so many shelters and safe houses that are waiting with open and protective arms, a doctor's office, or police officer, even a pastor or minister of a church. Really, you don't have to belong to that church, but if you happen to walk past a church and go in, I know someone will help you.

I don't know if you have a friend that you have confided in about your situation, but I know a true friend would not let you down and would truly want to help. I know you must protect yourself, and I also appreciate the fear you may be feeling about upsetting the beehive, because I was there, too! My only regret is that I waited so long before leaving.

But, as painful as it has been, I am so relieved I took that step of faith. Who knows what would have happened if I didn't? And like I said, it was my Lord Jesus that heard my cries and opened the doors protecting me, providing for me, and giving me that warrior courage to say, "No, no more!" And you know what? He hasn't left my side... not once!

I am now surrounded with my loving family that I was estranged from for over 20 years, church family, and new friends that are always encouraging. I want you to know that the Lord Jesus is very aware of your situation, and He is holding all the broken pieces of your life and He has plans to make something wonderfully good out of all those pieces.

I believe God wants us to be women of courage, displaying the beauty and strength of character that is filled with a worshipping heart, being kind and gentle and obedient to the Word of God. He loves you so much that He took on all the pain you are experiencing and more, and your broken life and the shameful direction you have been going in for so long is not the life He wants for you. Romans 10:11, says For the Scripture says, *"Whoever believes on Him will not be put to shame."* That, my friend, is living truth.

Just call on His name, right now, because He is ready to help you. I know you probably feel like you are locked in a prison, and no one knows, and you can't tell, because that is exactly how I felt for too long. And you may be feeling all alone, but I want you to know you are never alone. No, not ever! Jesus knows you are there, and He is watching and waiting to take your hand and lead you to safety!

We don't know each other, but can I be your friend? My heart is filled with much concern and sadness for you right now and I know God hears my prayers for you and He hears yours as well; I know He is reaching out to you and so many others right now. They say there are only two guarantees in life, death, and taxes. Well, I happen to know that is wrong.

You see, there are three guarantees... death, taxes, and Salvation through the blood of Christ Jesus that was shed for you and me, and for the whole world. All you have to do is accept that truth, call on His name, and reach out and grab onto His hand, and know, He will never let go of yours.

Remember, there is power in the name of Jesus! That's what He told me and that's what I believe because I have found it is true.

And if you are reading this book and you can say you are safe and secure in your relationship with your husband or boyfriend but know someone that is locked in the bondage I have been speaking of, maybe you could pray about how you could help that person to escape.

It may seem scary, getting involved with this kind of horror, but it is far worse allowing someone you know go through it and not do anything to help; knowing there was something you could have done but were too afraid or hesitant to get involved.

I know beyond a shadow of doubt that our God sees and hears, and He hears our prayers, your prayers, and prayer is what moves the hand of God. Anonymous calls don't cost much and your prayers, if only your prayers, are worth a lot to someone who needs help.

*"And we know that all things work
together for good to those who love God,
to those who are the called according to His purpose."*
Romans 8:28

Chapter 14

On My Knees

One of my most favorite, enjoyable, and encouraging pastime things to do is to take a book outside in my backyard patio and sit and read a true to life story! I truly believe every story, particularly the true ones, should have a happy ending, don't you? Now we all know that life is just not that way, no matter how we believe it is supposed to be. Then again, if it is a true event story, you also know it's not always going to have that ending that makes you want to cry tears of happiness while reaching for the Kleenex box!

I guess you can tell by the title of this new chapter, there hopefully will be that awaited happy ending, though it's going to take some serious Spiritual work, right?

Well, let's not get too far ahead of things, not just yet! I have a few things I want to share with you, so hang on.

It was about two or three years, after I had made my move from Hawaii to Reno, welcoming new beginnings including a new home, a long, too many years passed, awaited reunion with my parents and siblings, and new friends, that my daughter had called me to let me know her dad wasn't doing too well. She had been overseeing his needs, since I left, and was very aware of his physical and mental deterioration. He would soon be diagnosed with Alzheimer's and Mental illness, but the doctor said he has probably had lifelong Bipolar and Schizophrenia as well.

Wow, all the things I saw gradually worsening through the years and yet unable to do anything about. All those years trying to get him to the doctor, searching for someone to put the diagnosis to what I had suspected, has finally been voiced and recorded! She was pretty much drained from the final few years of his struggles.

With a quivering voice, she proceeded to say she didn't know how much longer he would live, as his health was greatly declining, and with tears she said, "Mom, I don't know who is going to want to stand up for him and speak, when he does die." Well, I have to be honest; my heart was not only breaking for her, but this news was so bittersweet!

Now, we know what the cause of so much pain was for all those years, for me and my children, not to mention extended family that turned a forever blind eye and just chalked it up to just his personality. This breaks my heart but also makes me so angry. How tragic, so very tragic. I cried for years, asking God why? Why did this life, this marriage have to end like this because it wasn't supposed to be like this? Then again, when I finally released it all into His hands, questions, and all, He gave me the peace and the courage to just keep my eyes on Him and continue moving forward.

Jesus is the answer; the only answer because I sure didn't have any, and no one else did either, except those who knew the Lord and they constantly redirected me back to Him. There's so much strength and hope in my relationship with Jesus. I can honestly say, I couldn't make it in life without Him and His comforting compassionate love.

I thought back to all those years, watching these illnesses slowly creep upon him, the constant waking me up in the middle of the night to ask me, "Where is the party that's going on?" and "Who are the kids playing behind your car?", at 2:30 in the morning. "Who is that old woman standing in the bathroom waving me to come to her?" That woman, I figured was his Grand Aunt who raised him and lived with us for 27 years before she finally died many years ago before he was seeing her in the bathroom!

The constant frustration of making doctor appointments, only for him to cancel them or not show up was so aggravating. Then, the many times I left work early just so I could join him when he did see the doctor. I felt it was so important we both hear what was happening to him and what the plan of help was going to be done, but to no avail! It was becoming so hopeless and futile.

I thought of all the sarcasm and temper explosions he'd throw at me for suggesting we see a doctor. Boy, what fight one person can hold within themselves. Just amazing! We all know death is expected for each one of us and with that comes the sobering truth of how we all have lived our lives, followed by deep thoughts of what will be next, especially for those who don't know Jesus Christ as their Lord and Savior! So, I continued to bang my knees, as I call it. They say (whoever they are) that prayer moves the hand of God, and I was counting on Him doing just that.

My husband had claimed to have accepted Jesus, back in the 70's, but there was always a conflict in his fruits. You know, when a person believes one thing but does the opposite? In Matthew 7:16, *"You will know them by their fruits. Do men gather grapes from thorn bushes or figs from thistles?"* Or as I have said many times, "you can't pick apples off a banana tree, and God does not keep company with the devil!"

My husband was quick to say he believed in Jesus as his Lord and Savior, and he read his Bible often. However, there was always that other person in him that was just plain opposite of a belief in Jesus and what the Bible teaches. Like I have said, it was as if he were two people, two different people, and as often as I tried to get him help, that plan always, always failed.

My heart went out to my daughter's concern, and I heard my voice saying, "I will do it. Don't worry." She immediately gasped, "Oh, thank you, Mom. You have no idea what a burden you just lifted off me!"

There had been just too much sorrow and pain in my life, my family's life with this man, and I was not about to let my daughter carry this all by herself. Needless to say, I continued to pray for this man, as I had for over four decades.

Yes, I continued to pray for my husband, however, it was the last two years before he passed away; I felt I wasn't praying deeply enough for him. So, I went before the Lord and just pleaded with all my heart, everything within me, that God would finally bring him to that breaking moment so he could finally understand how much he needed that personal knowing Jesus.

I remember before I left Hawaii, praying fervently for him, and one day the Lord had spoken to me through a vision and confirmed it through scripture.

In my vision, I saw him on a bed (somehow, I knew was a hospital bed, his death bed) and he had the white sheet pulled up to his shoulders. I was sitting at the foot of the bed on a chair just staring at him. I saw him trying to raise himself up with his elbows and he began saying, very excitedly, "Bev, Bev, now I know what you've been telling me all those years." It would be around that time reading my Bible that I read a scripture that jumped off the page at me. It was Psalm 12:5, *"For the oppression of the poor, for the sighing of the needy, Now I will arise, says, the Lord; I will set him in the safety for which he yearns."*

Then, again four months before he passed, the Lord gave me Psalm 41:3-4, *"The Lord will strengthen him on his bed of illness; you will sustain him on his sickbed."* I said, Lord, be merciful to me; Heal my *soul, for I have sinned against You."* I held onto these scriptures as I continued to pray for his salvation.

Then, one day I went before the Lord and asked something I had never done before. I asked, "Jesus, would You please put Your Love for him in my heart so I can pray more deeply and effectively for him." Oh, my goodness, you cannot imagine the power of praying in the Spirit, with such deep, deep focused advocacy and pure brokenness! The power, the draining, emptying out of your whole being, power in Jesus Love just slammed me down to my knees like I have never ever experienced before! I pleaded and projected this man up into the Lord's hands, advocating with all my heart, that he would be saved before Jesus took him.

It makes me cry when I look back on this time, even now as I write. Though, I truly felt the need to divorce him, I really didn't want to, but I had to escape his threats, because I knew he was capable of fulfilling what he was determined to do after four decades of marriage. Even so, there just makes no sense in the term divorce. Can you understand? This was still my husband, the 'death do us part' commitment I was always determined not to break, but finally I had to!

As he deteriorated and became more abusive, running away and walking down the highway too many times to count, leaving my daughter with sheer panic, the worry that someone wouldn't see him until it was too late and hit him with their car, needing to go search for him, unless a neighbor happened to see him and bring him home again. And the volatile moods that caused explosive rants, though he didn't really know what he was doing or saying, finally my daughter had to place him in a home, where he could get the 24/7 care that she was just not able to give any longer. He would soon develop a urinary infection that turned septic, running all through his body, and that is what finally took his last days to the end.

She shared with me most recently she was able to finally forgive him. It would be when he had violently grabbed her arm and growled "I want to kill you." Then, within seconds, he cried out, "I don't know why I said that! I don't know how to stop it!" It touched her heart so deeply, that suddenly compassion flowed over her, and she was filled with so much love for him, she felt like she finally had the dad she always wanted to love, and at that moment, she forgave him. She forgave him, finally!

She told me it was such a deep and heavy moment; she knew it was God working in her because she hadn't forgiven him yet, for all those years and she knew that's what Jesus wanted her to do, it was time!

About a week after this happened, she got the call to take him to the Care Home. The amazing thing is, there was no openings at this Care Home and wouldn't be for quite a while. She truly thought the doors opened when she was finally able to forgive her dad.

There was a moment during my conversation when there was a long silence and then crying. My daughter said though it made her deeply angry to have to recall the horror of her growing up years as I spoke about them, it was so helpful and needed to get all those memories as well as the locked up and hidden emotions, out and finally released. She said she had forgotten so much only because it had been suppressed for too long.

When I returned her attention to the moment his gun shot at the ceiling in our bedroom, going through the girls' bathroom wall, just missing them as they were getting ready for bed. The flood gates opened, and she gasped, "Oh, Mom, I almost forgot about that."

It happened during one of his rages directed to me. She said her sister had finished showering first and was dressing. Then, as she was getting out of the shower, she heard the gun shot and her sister pulled her to the floor covering her with her body to protect her. That night, as I tucked the girls into bed and spent a few moments loving on them and praying with them, was when my older daughter asked, "Mommy, is Daddy going to kill us tonight?" I cry just remembering that night, one of so many, many times.

It's amazing how we protect ourselves from the painful and hurtful things in life; we bury it, out of sight out of mind. That is, until it rises its ugly head only to bite again, only harder!

My daughter told me something I had never known before. She said she had begun having thoughts about, 'I'm going to have to hurt my Daddy so I can protect my Mommy.' I asked her what age she was when these thoughts started. She asked, "How old was I when I had the chickenpox?" I told her three and half years old. She said, "That's when I first had those thoughts, and they were always on my mind for years. I knew what he was doing and saying wasn't right. I didn't really know God yet. I just told Him, "I have to hurt my Daddy, because what he's doing to my Mommy isn't right." Can I tell you, she and I cried and cried!

These things had to come out for her, and it just breaks my heart to hear her tell me all this. Oh, my Lord Jesus, how much more is hidden? She told me again, she is so happy I am writing my story because she knows it's going to help someone... or many someone's. Why do children always have to pay!

Finally, five days before he passed, my older daughter called, who went to see her dad and felt the need to let me know he was already transitioning. His body was preparing to die. She asked, though I had forgiven him already, would I just talk to him and tell him just one more time? I said, "Of course, I will." She said, "Mom, he's in a coma and on oxygen." I told her, "Put the phone to his ear and I'll talk to him. He can hear me!"

Well, I spoke to him, not saying it was me, but of course, he knew it was. I said, "I know right now, you probably want to ask everyone for forgiveness, but I want you to know, everyone has already forgiven you. Your friends, your family, your children, and I have forgiven you, but I want you to know Jesus has forgiven you too, and He is standing right there at your side, holding out His hand to you. So, take it. He loves you and He wants to take you home with Him! Just let Him know you want to go with Him.

Then, I heard a soft voice gasp, "Oh my God"... and then

sobbing! So much sobbing! It was so soft and so meaningful. I covered the phone's speaker and began to cry. Then, my daughter took the phone and said, "He went back into the coma, Mom." I asked, "Was that him?" and she said, "Yes, Mom, he heard you." He heard you!

My heart still cries just remembering that moment, remembering those words. Now those daily tears are for joy... such grateful, unspeakably, thankful joy. This is my long-awaited gift. God's beautiful gift to me and I am so thankful, and I praise Him for it constantly. I am especially grateful because there was a time just before his infection became deadly, that he had been taken to the hospital for another infection.

Well, from what my daughter told me, all my children and most of my grandchildren were able to go to the hospital to see him. That's so important because that was when they were able to forgive him as well and let him know they loved him.

Funny, as I write, I'm suddenly remembering more details that I seemed to have packed away somewhere. When I say most of my grandchildren were able to visit him at the hospital, I now remember my daughter's youngest daughter wasn't able to visit.

You see, after that phone call telling me he was transitioning, my younger daughter who had been overseeing his care, called me to let me know I needed to pray for my granddaughter because she had been rushed to the hospital with severe pain in her stomach and they were soon going to do surgery on a tumor that was just found. She was 19 years old at the time.

With all this news, I had to get out of the house and just drive—somewhere, anywhere, or I was going to lose it. I got to the Christian bookstore and was just browsing, not really looking, or seeing anything. Soon, I would get another call saying, "Dad is soon going to pass, and he's having great difficulty breathing." Oh, the pain and deep sadness, watching someone approach the end of their life.

Minutes after that call, my younger daughter called and said that her daughter's surgery went well so she was on her way to see her dad. Once she arrived at the Care Home and spent only a few minutes with him (though he had just passed during her driving to see him), she was called back to the hospital as my granddaughter was coming out of surgery.

Within about 40 minutes, my daughter called again and said when she got to see her, my granddaughter said, "Mom, no more darkness." My daughter asked, "What do you mean? You're not having any more pain?" My granddaughter, with eyes still closed, still coming out of the anesthesia, and speaking slowly, "Papa is no more in darkness!" and then she went to sleep again. I get chills as I'm telling you this encounter.

How did she know he was gone? Did God tell her? Did she get to see her grandfather right after he passed? Oh my, I have no idea and no answers, and she doesn't remember that now. Just amazing!

At any rate, I believe now, you can say there was a happy ending. *"All things do work together for Good, to those who love God and are called according to His purpose"* (Romans 8:28). Halleluiah!

Now, you are probably wondering, 'what about her husband's memorial, and was a eulogy given?' Well, I was just getting to that. I certainly don't want to leave you hanging. Yes, it was written, but I did it before it was needed.

The day came in June 2018, five months before he died. I knew no one else would write it and I did promise my daughter I'd stand up for him. It's amazing what God can do in the depth of your heart when it's surrendered in submission. When you are able to lay everything down at His feet and say, Father thy Will be done, not mine!

God put His love for my husband into my heart and I set out, in complete defiance of all the evil the enemy purposed and wrote a four-page eulogy. Most everyone knew of his volatility, the short fuse to his anger, but I wanted to let people know, just who that other person was, the loving, kind, and fun person. I set out to reintroduce who he really was before life, illness, and unforgiveness destroyed him.

Sadly, I wasn't able to give the eulogy, however, the pastor who had spent many hours a day talking with him at the Care Home, did give it. Afterward, I thanked him for the gift he gave me by reading what my forgiving heart had written.

Can I tell you that God does hear our prayers and He answers all of them? He doesn't always answer how we want or when we expect it, but He truly hears and answers. I can also say I am surrounded by family and friends and precious church family whose love and concerned care has been such strength and I'm in constant contact with my children who have always stood by me. I think... no, I know that is what keeps me going. It's definitely the Lord who has caught and collected, not only all my tears, putting them in that bottle I've told you about, but Jesus continues to draw me nearer and nearer to Him every single day. Yes, I have truly been blessed!

As I mentioned, in 2015, while reading my daily devotionals, looking out my back sliding door, the Lord began to show me a very important message. It was a vision, but He also spoke to my heart. I call it **The Rocks**. I printed it out to share with my ladies in the Healed and Set Free study. You will notice, the way it's written, it's as if someone is talking to you telling this story, so read it and let it personally speak to you. I believe this message is so important and for everyone and that is why I am including it in my book. I hope you enjoy, and I pray it speaks to you as the Holy Spirit spoke it to me, as well as to all I have shared it with.

The Rocks

I want you to visualize a Path of Rocks and stare at it in your mind's eye. It's a Beautifully Scenic path. The skies are blue with beautifully shaped white clouds drifting across in silence, and just a wisp of breeze brushing over your face. The calm and peaceful moment relaxes your whole being. There are butterflies fluttering from one beautiful wildflower to the next on the right side of the path, and dragonflies are skipping gaily across the water on the left side of the path.

Now, take a deep breath… and watch as you walk along this path. You notice the rock under your feet is actually very tiny pebbles; so tiny, your feet leave a deep imprint with every step. Can you see it? As you walk, the pebbles soon become larger gravel and you are aware each step has the sound of crunching under your feet. Can you hear it? Soon, the crunching stops, and you are now walking on larger slippery river rock. Each step seems to cause your footing to become uneasy and slip as your ankle seems to twist, here and there, as you try to steady those steps. Can you feel it?

Then, all of a sudden, you are facing very large boulders. As you gaze upon them, you are puzzled, and immediately stop. You look at those massive boulders and wonder, 'how on earth am I going to get up over those things? I can't even climb up on them, much less walk on them.' Your head lowers in defeat and your heart becomes drenched in failure and discouragement. Then you hear a loud yelling cry, fly out of the deepest inner most part of your gut, "Lord, how am I supposed to follow You up this Mountain…. while carrying all this baggage!?!"

You can almost hear the stillness of that defeat! Then, an incredibly, soothingly, sweet Voice speaks with such power and authority, it commands attention, "Give it to Me, I'll carry it for you!" Suddenly, you know, deep within your heart, Who it is, that's speaking, Who Knows your Name. As you listen, tears fill your eyes to overflowing and then gently slide down your cheeks.

You take notice that, He didn't say, "Why did you bring all

that baggage"? He didn't ask, "Why didn't you leave it behind?"
And, He didn't say, "I don't know why you thought you could
carry it in your own strength!" No. No! He said, "Give it to Me,
I'll carry it for you!"

What did you see? What do you understand about what you just saw?

This was a vision I had in 2015. While reading my devotional, I was allowing all my brokenness to circle around me, having no answers and totally crying out to Jesus. This is what, I truly believe, the Holy Spirit showed me and was speaking to my heart!

Each layer of rock represents all the different types of worry, fear, unforgiveness, regret and crushing heartache. Some were very small, almost miniscule, like failed plans and broken promises, all leaving me with helplessness.

Then, there were the others, the shatteringly horrendous kind; you can probably picture those for yourself! These are the kind that we hide deep within the pit Satan has deceivingly drawn you and I to dig so we can bury those burdens out of sight. Out of sight, out of mind, right?

It's as if these burdens have become a large blanket, all created by the enemy. And sadly, those times we wiggle into that blanket, in order to feel warmth and security, though it is false… Nobody can see or know… and eventually we soon discover that wiggling causes us to plunge deeper into that Pit. And all that time… Jesus is standing, watching, and waiting for you to cry out and lay it all down at His Feet. He paid for it, every one of those burdens, and yet we tend to keep a tight grip on them. Why... And for What?

This letting go, and laying everything at His feet, is God's Will for us and I truly believe we are living at a time—so close to His return—that He wants you and me, His Bride, to let go of anything and everything that is hindering our walk. In other words, He wants our hands free... Totally Free! You know why? When we see Him, we are going to have the empty hands needed to raise up and Praise His Name.

We need to understand, we can't receive our healing, until we have forgiven! We can't forgive until we give it... Lay it at His Feet. And we can't give it without seeing it... Calling it out from where we buried it and calling it by name!

As for my daughter, when I mentioned I was writing my story, she asked if I would mention the effects of Alzheimer's, not just the debilitating stages for the patient but the devastating effects this disease has on the loved ones, not to mention how draining and tremendously painful and difficult it is to watch that loved one, who was once so vivacious and active, just fade away.

These affects also apply to mental illness and how it takes such a tight grip on our loved one and doesn't want to let go. It truly takes a courageous heart and great mental strength to care for their deteriorating loved ones and it is extremely important to do research on the diseases and the early symptoms, as well as planning ahead for the care that will be needed. No one should have to go through this alone, and remember the caregivers need help, too!

There are organizations as well as doctors, care homes and hospice facilities that have resources available for the asking. Do yourself favor and plan a head. You can also call the National Helpline for Alzheimer's 1-800-272-3900.

I would also like to share something about my daughter, and feel free to do so, as she considers her life a testimony and huge blessing of God's Love. For many reasons, we aren't even completely sure of, but because of the huge battle she fought, while standing by her dad and caring for him through such dark and agonizing days, the mental and physical pressure that took such a toll on her, she would go through an experience that should have been her death as well, just seven months after her dad passed.

Because of this, my daughter literally went through moments other people have reported during their own "after death" experience. She remembers her gurney being rolled into the ER and though her mind was foggy, within moments she saw the softest, brightest light begin to shine all around her. Then she saw her dad, who had died seven months before, come out of some clouds just above her head. He knelt down on one knee beside her gurney and said, "Kelly, take my hand. Don't worry, I've got you."

All of a sudden, someone yelled, "Administered" (medication that gave her only a 50/50 chance of surviving), and then she felt her gurney moving really fast (toward the CT scan). As the nurses swiftly moved her down the hall, her dad followed closely looking down at her. As they made eye contact, she noticed he was suddenly becoming farther away. It was at that moment she knew it wasn't her time to go. She said she couldn't remember anything else after that.

She has completely baffled the doctors, who still shake their heads as they exclaim, she should not even be here today. It was first thought she was having a stroke because of the extreme symptoms and though the doctors were sure, the clot was never found. She has been diagnosed with a rare Complex Migraine with Aura, of which still plagues her when she is under any stress.

Whatever you want to call it and whether anyone wants to believe it or not, what she saw will forever be indelible in her heart and memory forever. This was truly God's Grace.

I tell you this because now, what she experienced has brought her closer to God and now she says she truly knows Jesus, in a way she never knew Him before. Her relationship is powerfully real and close, and she shares Jesus with whoever will listen, everywhere she goes.

You see, when she was four years old, we came home from church, one of the few times we ever went, and while I was making lunch for the family, she walked into the kitchen and said, "Mommy, I want Jesus in my heart, and I want Him in my heart right now!"

I immediately called the pastor at that church and asked him to come over and talk to her or us, just talk, as I didn't know who else to call. I felt this was so unusual for someone so young and I wanted to know more. He came, and after talking with her, to this day, I'm not sure what was spoken, but he came back into the kitchen and said with a big grin, "Well, she sure knows what she wants."

The following Sunday, she, and the pastor's four-year-old and another four-year-old, walked forward at church to accept Jesus as their Lord and Savior. They would be Baptized the following Sunday at the beach. Years went by and life happens, as we can all attest to, and I began praying many years ago, that four-year-old would come back to Jesus!

Little did I or anyone else know that is what happened, and it would take the situation with her dad, to awaken that 'come back.' She, as I praise our Lord Jesus, who is so faithful, longsuffering, and merciful. I just thought someone might want to hear that story.

Today, I can hold my head high and truly say my life has become full. Since I gave Jesus all my baggage, all my pain, and my whole life, He not only took it, but He is also using it to serve at my church through teaching Bible Studies, as well as counseling the broken, those who need someone to come along side of them and say, "Give me your arm, I'll walk with you."

My passion is counseling other women who are going through the destructive ravages of abuse, as my heart grieves with them because I've been there. The Lord has given all of us many gifts, and I have come to realize one of mine is Comforter and I stand on 2 Corinthians 1:3-4, *"Blessed be the God and Father of our Lord Jesus Christ, the Father of mercies and God of all comfort, who comforts us in all our tribulation, that we may be able to comfort those who are in any trouble, with the comfort with which we ourselves are comforted by God."*

Now, as I come to the close of my story, my greatest advice to anyone reading this and to anyone who would listen, I want you to know just how great our God is. His mercy and grace and His love are so huge. There are two things I hope you will hold onto and keep ever so close to your heart and that is forgiveness and prayer.

Forgiveness is Jesus, the Son of God, Who paid our debt so we can have salvation and look forward to being with Him in Heaven forever one day. And prayer is the most powerful gift God has given us. He hears prayer and He answers prayer so don't ever, ever stop praying for your loved ones, family and friends, no matter how long it takes to receive an answer. After all, it took 43 years to receive my answer, my gift. He may not answer the way you want or expect, but His timing is all His, and it's always on time and perfect. Remember, 1 Thessalonians 5:17, *"Pray without ceasing."* He hears you!

May I encourage you, take heart and don't give up, and don't let go of Jesus hand no matter what. And if you don't know my Lord yet, call out to Him because He will hear you. Ask Him to open the eyes of your heart that you can see what He sees in you, a precious life that's worth more than you could ever know. He sees you and He's waiting to fill you with a love you have never known before, a love greater than anyone else has ever offered you. A love, Who gave His life just for you because you are worth it.

To all who mourn in Israel he will give: beauty for ashes; joy
instead of mourning; praise instead of heaviness.
Isaiah 61:3

Chapter 15

No More Ashes

Now that I have made the decision to move in pouring out my life story within these pages of transparency, my desire is to reach out to any broken heart that may need to hear. Oh, there is hope; there are definite answers for your healing!

As I look back over all the years of broken dreams, the crumbs and miniscule eggshells left over from a distorted picture of marital bliss, I can't help but wonder why we even want to travel on a path that leads to failure, lies and just ugly sinfulness. I would like to believe we originally set out in a direction that leads to Gods promised fulfillment, but somehow, somewhere, we seem to make a dreadful mistake by taking a wrong turn, and in doing so, we find ourselves running toward Satan's disguised and dangled trinkets of poisonous venom of sin. His very best of evil and corrupt pleasure that only brings darkness, shame and confusion, dishonoring our Great God who instituted something so beautiful; His gift to us!

Why do we fall for that? I'm once again reminded, "We are such stupid dumb sheep." Yes, oh yes we are, and how desperately we need our Shepherd, our Savior's help and guidance! My heart breaks all over again when I think of all the countless times "I wished I would've, could've, and should've!" Anyone on board with that regret?

I believe we all must face those wrong decisions and mistakes of our past and know we can't go back! I'm facing it now and have a strong hunch you may be as well. Wouldn't it be wonderful if we could erase the blackboard of our lives? Wait, do we even have blackboards any longer? Maybe, dry erase boards are the correct terminology of today.

At any rate, there's only One who can make a difference, and His name is Jesus! He continually stands by, just watching and waiting for us to want His help; to cry out in desperation, wanting the transforming beautiful life He has planned for us. I have learned that now, and hope and pray you have as well.

We all have those tainted mountains in our background and though we don't really forget them, He does... when we ask Him to. He will use them, however to redirect our path back to Him. You just have to believe that, and if there are any doubts, please call out! He's listening, I can promise you that.

Another thing about forgetting is something I have learned through His counseling and guidance. You see, it all starts with facing those difficult, painful and what we think is unforgivable regrets. We so often want to bury it and move on. The problem with that thinking is that it doesn't get removed from our hearts. Oh no, it follows us because we, we are so smart, are very much aware of where we locked it away. Ah ha, yep! It's almost like making a patchwork quilt of remembrances of our lives.

There was a moment, when I had taken a step back and look into my mirrored past; I realized my life could be likened to that quilt. It's as if each distinct square of fabric represented one of my memories. Some heartwarming and wonderfully happy, some very sad, cruel and hurtful, and as each piece is carefully arranged and placed in a purposeful order, it is done so with both loving thoughts and painful remembrances. Once the quilt pieces had been sewn together, it represented the fabric of my Faith Walk.

Then, as I put my needle down and took a long look at my work, I realized I couldn't just cut out the squares I didn't like or no longer wanted to be reminded of, because it would only leave a gaping hole, a hole that would eventually have to be filled... either by the warmth of love or with more... maybe unbearable sadness or regret and I couldn't possibly know for sure of which.

You see, that filling is lovingly held in the hands of Jesus, as I knew He was walking beside me; as I know He is walking beside you. And as He does so, He is leading you and I on the Exquisite Path He has planned for, watching over us as new memories are given permission to be formed in our Life's Walk of Faith... in our Quilt of Life as I like to call it.

I have also learned, if I refuse to face these horrible, ungodly, and painful feelings and experiences, it will only crush my heart all over again...and again and again! I realized I had to deal with them and so do you, my friend. That's the first step that leads us all to Jesus for that healing we so desperately want and need, facing it, then laying it down at His feet. You may want to ask, 'Is that it? Is that all I have to do?' Oh no, that's only the beginning, sister, but it's the greatest start.

Now, there is another huge mountain you will have to face, and that is of forgiveness. Forgiveness not just for the one who harmed you, but for yourself! You may be thinking, 'Oh no, the most difficult assignment of all!' Yes, but you can do it. Like I have always believed, if I can do it, you can as well. I can attest to that truth; you want to know why? It only takes a mustard seed full, as well as a 'want to!'

Forgiveness! Oh, I seem to have such small comprehensive understanding sometimes, when I look at that truth. And at the same time, while looking back at all I'd done, the messes I created and huge mistakes I'd gotten myself into, the choices I've made that led me onto a path of sin and brokenness, knowingly or not, and just plain, all my failures. I know we all are guilty of all those things and more. But I was faced with the need to put on glasses of sharper clarity and believe what He says about forgiveness. I had to face the Cross!

I had to visualize every lash of that whip embedded with metal and glass that tore His flesh open, the piercing of those thorns being crushed into His head, the sharp force of that sword being driven into His side, every strike of that hammer that nailed Him to that Cross with the weight of my sin, it was because you and I were truly worth it! Taking a fixed stare at Him in my place on that Cross left me breathless, and I only hope you are able take a long, hard look and let what you see take your breath away as well.

He died for ALL sin… the ones I acknowledged and confessed to, and the ones I had placed under lock and key, deep within the Pit of "I can't forgive myself." Forgive myself? Yeah, that person who needs your forgiveness just might be YOU. Did you hear that? You see, forgiveness is handing the justice over to God. You know why? Because there is a very, very powerful scripture in Hebrews 10:31, *"It is a fearful thing to fall into the hands of the living God."* He deals with it and sees to it that you get your justice… but it's His work and in His timing, not yours! We need to remember justice and vengeance belong to Him.

Also, remember, when we give that person to God through forgiveness, or when we open our hearts up to Him, lying all bare before Him, something very important takes place. His loving and forgiving power takes over and moves within His Mercy and Grace.

I forgave my abuser, my husband, but now I had to forgive ME! That was a huge hurdle for sure. I knew I couldn't hide behind "me", by withholding or refusing to face the fact I was included in this picture as well. I had to remember, forgiveness is not an emotion or even a feeling, and it does not mean just because you forgave, you need to return to the stronghold God has released you from. Who in their right mind wants to remain chained to their past, the pain and atrociousness of yuk, right?

I realize many get forgiveness mixed up with going back into the boiling pot that once scorched you. I had to ask myself, 'What do you plan to do with that load of 'Nobody knows but me' heavy burden; you keep hiding behind you, Bev? And may I ask, for what benefit?' After all, remembering and holding onto all that yuk is only beneficial when it reminds us of the extent of God's forgiveness. And while I was confronting "me", I had to ask 'What Did God send His Only Begotten, Precious Sinless Son to the Cross for, anyway? Isn't that heavy load getting heavier to carry? Is it preventing you from receiving all our Precious Lord wants you to have?'

I have to admit, I heard what I was saying to "me" deep down, and I knew it was true. Again, I asked "me" as I am asking you (if you know the Lord already), 'Why are you looking at the water? You know the water Peter was so sure he could walk on?' Jesus doesn't want you to stare at the water. He wants you to get your staring gaze onto Him!

Jesus gave His life and shed His blood, that you and I could be saved and set free from ALL sin. He didn't have to, but wanted to, all because we couldn't save ourselves. His love for us is beyond comprehension. It's almost too big to take in, and yet all He asks is, "Believe it!"

You see, I am not capable of helping myself in anything that is of value, because my attempts, within myself are fruitless and pathetic! We need to know; the enemy is very savvy to what stirs us up. He knows our fears, insecurities, weaknesses, and our struggles. He knows a lot about us and will do anything he can to get us to fail and not believe what Jesus did for us on that Cross.

We also need to be reminded that Satan is out for our total ruin and complete destruction. Remember what John 10:10 says, *"The thief comes only to steal and kill and destroy; I have come that they may have life, and have it to the full."*

You need to know you are strong... stronger than you may feel or want to believe right now. But, let that "Lion" out of its cage and let the courageous strength that He can and will give you rush to the surface, and then just Roar! Remember, when you are weak, He is your strength, I can promise you that! None of us have the power within ourselves, to heal or forgive, or even fix us, only He can. He wants to work a beautiful newness in us all and just know, He will continue doing so until the day we meet Him face to face. All we need to do is let go and surrender to Him!

Oh, and the forgetting part, I touched on earlier? You need to know as I found out, that 'forgetting thing' may seem like an impossibility at first glance, but there is a beautifully lined piece of tapestry sewn within that square of fabric that goes into your Quilt of Life.

So many women have dealt with some type of heartbreak and cruelty, whether within their marriages or just life itself. But, no matter what that broken piece represents, it all has the same remedy, and that is laying it at Jesus feet, forgiving your "hurter", whether it's you or someone else, and putting your eyes on the only one who can help you by taking the meaning of pain out of your 'forget' and turning it into something more beautiful.

I can honestly say, I really thought I was doomed to having a covering of pain and regret wrapped around me the rest of my life. However, though it took a few years, I realized I could talk about what happened without feeling the pain. Does that make any sense to you?

At first, if someone asked me about my life, I felt so horrible to have to return to what I felt I was trying to forget. But then, in keeping my eyes on my Lord, reading my Bible, and getting involved with church and reaching out to other ladies, especially those who shared my life story, I found I could talk about it without the pain. It no longer held me in the grips of control! Only the Lord Jesus can do that! That memory piece becomes farther and farther away from your Memory of Importance! No more attachment, **no more ashes**!

My beautiful sisters, open the eyes of your heart, so you are able to see what He sees in you… a Beautiful Diamond created by His hand. We have so tarnished ourselves with our wrong and wayward decisions, our failures, the paths we have mistakenly walked throughout our lives, the relationships that waved that red flag in front of us, yet we ignored for whatever reason. That voice within everyone's heart that whispers what He wants for us, the best direction for us and yet, again we suppress that voice and ignore it.

We all have turned aside so many times to do our own will. May we focus on a desire for Him and His Will and plan for us, as we each say, "I will forgive that one; I will forgive me, Lord." I pray you truly want Him to make the changes in you, that only He knows is perfect and then watch as He chisels away and sands off all your imposed imperfections.

May you see yourself imperfectly perfect, knowing He is making you more like Jesus, knowing His wise and loving hands are continually reshaping and remolding all of us to be more like Him. You see, my sisters, He isn't finished with you yet, and we need to understand the beautiful labor of love never rushes... it always takes time, patient time, His timing!

"Today, if you will hear His voice, Do not harden your hearts."
Hebrews 4:7

Chapter 16

It's All About Jesus

My, at one time and "for more than half my life" other half—who was also "the other half of my heart"—is no longer, and now my heart has been set completely free. Free from torment and anguish that had locked him in a world of a progressive illness and wouldn't take its claws off him until his end... but God! But God had the keys and heard my voice. It's as if the Lord said, "No, he's mine because "the other half of his heart" never gave up her quest in approaching My throne; her determined pleading for his release into Heaven!"

Mental illness robs its victim and loved ones of such irreplaceable life treasures, in relationships. That illness is, I

Within the Shadow of "I Do"

believe one of Satan's tools to, *"kill, steal and destroy"*, John 10:10. But God... Only He can restore and save!

Don't stop praying, dear hearts! God hears your heart, and He is collecting all your tears, just like I have previously told you. And remember, Joel 2:25, *"So I will restore to you the years that the swarming locust has eaten."* It's a Promise!

It is so heartbreaking, the deep and wasted tragedy of living within this illness, watching a loved one being destroyed, just like the locusts manage to attack the crops of life with their destruction... but God! He has the last say and those crops of life will not only be restored, but His breath will breathe new life into them. You can count on it because He said so!

Our Lord Jesus, through His willingness to go to the Cross, who laid His life down for all mankind, paying our debt because we couldn't, has conquered all evil. He conquered, so when we accept what He did for us, purely out of Agape Love—His highest Love—we are more than conquerors and He has won this huge battle in my life. I cannot thank Him enough because I couldn't make it in life without Him.

I began to realize, back in 2017, that had I not gone through all that I have; had I not surrendered my life into His hands, I wouldn't have the personal relationship with my Lord that I have now. I miss my children and I'm heartsick over missing out on watching my great-grandchildren, not only coming into this world, but watching them grow. To know they really don't know me makes my heart sad, yet I cling to that scripture in Joel 2:25, and know my Lord understands and will restore such joy one day.

Now, I focus on lifting my children and their children up to Him, believing He will gather them and save them as well, as they see the need to surrender to the Son of God, our Lord and Savior. I count on Him to save them just like He did their dad! He hears our desperate cries, "Lord, take the scales off their heart's eyes so they may see their dire need for You. Cause them to know You are the answer, the Only answer, and You hold the keys to their freedom because Jesus paid for it!"

I want you to know, this book of my mine—my story—is not just all about me and what I, my family, my husband, my marriage went through. No, my purpose was to bring attention to the countless women who are crushed under the hand of abuse. I often say and truly believe, the silence within our churches, communities, and families, is screaming for help in this matter!

I know there may be some who would say, 'I don't hear it. I don't know what you're talking about.' Perhaps they aren't listening or even paying attention, but those voices are there. I know, because I have counseled so many who have admitted they thought they were alone and no one else was going through what they were, are or have. I have counseled many who cried when they realized they weren't the only one experiencing such

177

brutality.

Yes, I know, because I was one of them. It takes huge courage and strength to stand up and say, "No, you can't hurt me anymore," or stand up with all bravery and announce, "I am a victim."

No one enjoys sharing their, so called, dirty laundry, but God bless the women who are brave enough to stand. God bless all who hear them, and are willing to help, even if it was the woman who got herself into this situation. But more importantly, praise to our Lord that He is watching, listening, and doing something about those cries!

You must know, it's really all about Jesus, and what He does with all our broken pieces of life. He has all our broken and ugly pieces and He's making something beautiful, something to Glorify His name.

I'm reminded, when I first set out to write my story, that I was completely broken, too. But, as my Lord guided and directed His path for me, He was also remolding and creating a new and clean heart in me, to be used one day. As I'm writing this, it has occurred to me that I neglected to mention some interesting facts about my health.

During the lengthy stress I had endured over the years in my marriage, I had eventually broken six teeth. That was a gradual breaking because of my unavoidable clinching my teeth during the nights. At any rate, I have been able to get that problem fixed through implants. Such a costly, lengthy, and painful procedure, to say the least. But now I have the teeth needed to eat properly. I know there are many with that problem and because of the cost, they aren't able to have it done. However, I am so grateful I was provided a way to go through the procedure.

Another situation I encountered six years after relocating to my new home, was chest pain... out of the blue! I found myself in the ICU for three days because of Takotsubo Cardiomyopathy, or another name is 'broken heart syndrome.' Takotsubo cardiomyopathy is a weakening of the left ventricle, the heart's main pumping chamber, usually as the result of severe emotional or physical stress.

As a nurse, I was familiar with this interesting condition, but it never occurred to me that I could possibly be one who would experience it. But it's not supposed to happen again, so I'm told, and medication is seeing to that. It will show up on an EKG as a heart attack, but it's not. Then again, there are always two opinions in the medical field. But no matter the opinions, I truly feel I had suffered "a broken heart."

Now, as I have experienced His new remolding, His fixing me, all because I have asked Him to, and He did, as He saw the need. My eyes have begun to be fixated only on Him, and He has heard my heartfelt request; my request, if I am to reveal this painful story, to place myself into the scrutiny of others, let me do so with my eyes on You, Lord. I ask that You get All the Glory for what You have done with my... our broken lives, our mess! It's all about You, Jesus... It's ALL about You!

Remember that we are stupid, dumb sheep who need the guiding hand and watchful eye of a loving and caring Shepherd. We so often chart our own course, thinking He's not looking, or we think He won't care, because we know what's best for us, right? Then, when we do go our own way, we soon find we are lost and have made a mess of things and our lives. Then, when we realize we can't fix us, we cry out, "Lord help me, I'm drowning in my carelessness."

We need to trust our Lord in the plan He has for us and in doing so, get our eyes off the water, like Peter in Matthew 14:29-30. Peter wanted to walk to Jesus on the water, but soon his eyes focused on the blustery wind and the water, and then he sunk... crying out, *"Lord, help me."* We need to trust Him and it's all by faith.

I'm continually reminded of the man in Mark 9:24. When Jesus asked him if he believed that his son could be healed, the man said, *"Yes, I believe, but help my unbelief."* Isn't this where we find ourselves many times?

Yes, Jesus does what His love does; He pulls us to safety time and again. When will we ever let go of our determined wills and let God! We so desperately need to understand, Jesus wants a personal, very personal relationship with you and me. You see, it's not enough to just believe He exists! He wants us to know Him; to know He is our Shepherd, our Savior, and our only true God! And when you do realize He is holding your hand and won't let go, you will understand He is as close as the next breath, the breath He gave you to breathe!

Oh Lord, my prayer is for everyone who would care to read this book, that Your great love and anointed presence will flow over them, filling them with renewed hope and trust in You. Give them Your courage to stand in Your presence knowing the great sacrifice You paid just for them. Let them experience Your perfect Peace and incredible Joy as they are assured every step of their way is because of Your perfect plan for them, and that You are working out all the details and choreographing their every step, providing every need for their blessing, in Jesus' name!

Thank you from the bottom of my heart!

TELL ME YOUR STORY
By Beverly Chong

Tell me your story; I know you must have one.
As women, we all do, especially the unspoken ones.
The pain you have purposed and determined to hide,
The scars so dressed up, yet won't be permitted to lie.

Tell me your story.
I need to know I'm not alone.
Is your heart drowning in tears, too?
Carefully hidden; not allowed to be shown.

Do you own a blanket of guilt and filthy shame?
Displaying the raw truth of reckless or imposed blame.
You've draped it over your shoulders, a sign of reprimand.
Oh, please tell me, you do understand!

Did He, as with me, guide you to the water?
And when you cried out, oh please tell me you did too.
Did He, as with me, lovingly whisper...
"Don't you know, my precious child, I've got you?"

If you feel I'm telling your story,
As I'm convinced, you're telling mine
Let's cry our tears together
As I know we shall heal in due time.

You see, we all have a story
Filled with wrong turns, broken pieces, and heartache.
But if we take courage to lay all our mess at His feet,
He will finish that story and make it Beautiful...
All for His Name's sake. **(2 Corinthians 1:3-4)**

Coming Soon
Watch for Beverly's new Children's book,
"Gretchen's Gift
A Royally Enchanting Journey"
Coming December 2021

Dear Reader-
If you have any questions about my story;
if you've been suffering with emotional pain from the
hardships of abuse; if you need prayer,
guidance, direction or encouragement,
Or you want to know more about Jesus Christ
and how much He loves you,
I am here for you,
To God be the glory.

Contact Information:
Beverly Chong
Certified Christian Counselor
rraininhim@gmail.com

"For I will restore health to you
and heal you of your wounds," says the Lord.
(Jeremiah 30:17)